14.99

KT-216-079

TES Management Guide for Heads and Senior Staff

30130504059282

c/R
STZ.
o/R
s/97
37/8/2012
TES

TES Management Guide for Heads and Senior Staff

Archimedes

E0004695059001.

Butterworth-Heinemann
Linacre House, Jordan Hill, Oxford OX2 8DP
A division of Reed Educational and Professional Publishing Ltd

ℛ A member of the Reed Elsevier plc group

OXFORD   BOSTON   JOHANNESBURG
MELBOURNE   NEW DELHI   SINGAPORE

First published 1996

© Archimedes 1996

All rights reserved. No part of this publication
may be reproduced in any material form (including
photocopying or storing in any medium by electronic
means and whether or not transiently or incidentally
to some other use of this publication) without the
written permission of the copyright holder except
in accordance with the provisions of the Copyright,
Designs and Patents Act 1988 or under the terms of a
licence issued by the Copyright Licensing Agency Ltd,
90 Tottenham Court Road, London, England W1P 9HE.
Applications for the copyright holder's written permission
to reproduce any part of this publication should be addressed
to the publishers

British Library Cataloguing in Publication Data
Archimedes
   TES management guide for heads and senior staff
   1   School management and organization – Great Britain
   2   School management teams
   I   Title   II   Guide for headteachers and senior staff   III   The
   Times Educational Supplement
   371.2'07'0941

ISBN 0 7506 2802 2

Composition by Scribe Design, Gillingham, Kent, UK
Printed and bound in Great Britain by
Biddles Ltd, Guildford and King's Lynn

Contents

Introduction

In 1989, I was invited to write what might be called an agony column on the school management page of the *Times Educational Supplement*. I thought that this was an interesting idea, which might possibly run for a few months, but I felt sure that it would not be very long before I ran out of fresh questions to answer and new topics to address. Seven years on, it is still running.

In part, we have Her Majesty's Government to thank for this. Over that same period, the schools of Britain have been bombarded with a bewildering succession of initiatives, reforms and regulations on a scale that would have broken the backs of less resilient institutions. Those responsible for leading and managing schools have needed all the help they can get and the TES has played its part in offering that help.

The column has not just dealt with laws and regulations. It is true that many questions have sought elucidation on that score, but the answers have been more to do with management in the context of the legal framework rather than simply spelling out the bare facts.

The column has ranged widely, responding to whatever has moved correspondents to write. This book is a collection of the questions and answers, reassembled under the headings of the most important topics, a selection which reflects the preoccupations of the teaching profession during its most turbulent period. A few answers have been updated, where the law has changed since they were first written, but most remain unchanged, like the essential task of good management which underlies them all.

Why Archimedes? Forty years ago, a young and enthusiastic Latin master believed he might enhance his class's awareness of the ancient world by giving each pupil a classical pseudonym. Some were easy, straight translations of their names – Dyke, I recall, was known as 'Fossa' – while others were related to physical characteristics, such as ginger hair. The habitual latecomer was 'Cunctator'. One boy was caught doodling with his compasses, when he should have been concentrating on Kennedy's 'Shortbread Eating Primer' (there wasn't a single copy which did not bear this carefully amended title), and so 'Archimedes' was reborn. Forty years on, when a pseudonym was needed for another purpose, it was the obvious choice.

The readers of this book may not have occasion to cry 'Eureka'. There are no great discoveries here, but I hope that it may provide both help and comfort in a troubled and complicated educational world.

Archimedes

1
The teacher's job

Many of the questions I have received have related to the duties and rights of teachers. Heads and Deputies write to ask how far their authority extends, while other teachers have wanted to know whether what they are being required to do is acceptable or not.

Since 1987, most of these questions have been easier to answer than they were previously. The duties of a teacher are set out very plainly in the *School Teachers' Pay and Conditions of Service Document* and, although the document is revised annually to take account of new pay awards, the duties themselves have changed little. This is not, perhaps, surprising, because the original version owed much to the work of a working party of representatives of teachers and employers which met under the aegis of ACAS in the dying days of the old Burnham Committee. In other words, the document incorporates, by and large, what both sides thought was a reasonable definition of the teacher's job.

A key feature of the document, from the unions' point of view, was the definition, for the first time, of the time limits set upon teachers' work. It was laid down that teachers were required to work under the direction of their Head for 195 days in the year for a total time which should not exceed 1265 hours.

In the early days, many people thought that both employers and teachers would become 'clock-watchers' and that the professionalism of teachers would disappear. Fortunately, this did not happen and issues relating to 195 days and 1265 hours do not come up very often. They remain important psychologically, however, because, as my correspondence shows, teachers are much more conscious than they used to be that they cannot be required to do anything which a Head may choose to demand of them.

For Heads and Deputies, however, these constraints did not apply and, while they did not want them at the time, there are occasions when Deputies in particular look a little enviously at the protection which their junior colleagues enjoy.

Although the definition of duties is very thorough, not everything is covered: the duty of loyalty remains implicit.

Q. Is it acceptable for an LEA to insist that all teachers must obtain prior approval for any publication of material related to local educational matters?

A. If the assistant in the local butcher's shop wrote to the paper to say that his employer was selling poor quality meat, what would one expect would happen to him? Rules of the kind you quote are a reminder that every employee has an implied contractual duty of loyalty to his employer which, if breached, may lead to retribution. Whether it is a good idea for an employer to seek to protect both himself and his employee by making rules to prevent the possibility of such a breach is a matter of personal judgement. Some LEAs take this step because they fear that teachers, being on the whole politically as well as educationally aware, may cause them political damage by what they write. One may argue that this would be a good thing but, for an individual teacher, it conflicts with the duty of loyalty. The legitimate way around the difficulty is to have one's views expressed through one's union: material written on behalf of a union is not subject to the employer's constraint.

One of the trickiest issues arises whenever teachers are asked to do something outside the school's territory. Matters relating to school journeys are dealt with in Chapter 15, but this hardy perennial belongs here.

Q. What is the legal position of teachers who supervise pupils boarding buses outside the school?

A. Their position is the same as it is at any other time when they are supervising pupils, namely that they have a duty to exercise the degree of care and supervision which might be expected of a reasonable parent. When the bus queue is actually on school premises, there are no other issues involved. When the pupils are outside the school and on the public highway, other considerations arise, not least because of the dangers of traffic and the possibility of the involvement of members of the public who happen to be passing. Under no circumstances should a teacher ever attempt to give directions to traffic or to members of the public: to do so is to accept responsibility for any untoward consequences of that intervention. The presence of a teacher ostensibly in charge of the pupils means that he or she is, to some extent, accepting responsibility for their behaviour and this, in the particular circumstances, could be rather more extensive than when they are inside the school.

Having said that, I am well aware that there are hundreds of schools up and down the country where the orderly boarding of buses outside schools is only possible because teachers are present to supervise. It is essential for the safety of pupils and public alike that this should be so and it is one of the many examples of the duties which teachers undertake outside their classrooms and which receive scant recognition.

Sometimes, this kind of duty can be even more demanding:

Q. Our school playing field is separated from the buildings by a busy road. There is a light-controlled crossing. Can the Head direct teachers to supervise pupils crossing that road and does this place the teachers in a vulnerable position, if an accident occurs?

A. There are many and various occasions where teachers are required to supervise pupils off school premises, including, of course, all school trips and field-work. This case differs from others only in that it is a regular requirement. The Head is probably acting in accordance with the wishes of parents, who should know about this aspect of the school programme, and with common sense in directing staff to supervise pupils using the crossing, rather than letting them make their own way.

So long as the staff confine themselves solely to supervising the pupils – and with a light-controlled crossing, there should be no question of attempting to direct road traffic – they are no more vulnerable to a charge of negligence than they are elsewhere. If a teacher instructed or encouraged a pupil to cross against the lights, that would be both irresponsible and negligent. If a pupil did that in spite of being told not to, the teacher is unlikely to be held responsible.

Whether the Head is acting reasonably in requiring this duty of the staff is a matter which can only be judged on the merits of the particular circumstances. A teacher who believes that a direction is unreasonable has the right to challenge it through the grievance procedure.

Another aspect of teachers' conduct, which is not covered by the Document, is their general conduct, including the way in which they present themselves for work.

Q. What is the legal standing of a code of conduct for teachers adopted by the governors alongside their new disciplinary and grievance procedures?

A. The governors are fully entitled to draw up such a code of conduct and to expect teachers at the school to comply with it.

Failure to do so could lead to disciplinary procedure against which the only viable defence, assuming the breach to be established, would be that the requirements of the code of conduct were unreasonable.

One would expect that a governing body that wished to draw up such a code would do so after consultation with the staff and would thereafter make it known to teachers seeking appointment at the school. Failure to agree on the part of the staff is not an obstacle to implementing the code, although it is clearly preferable to obtain consent if possible.

Q. Having read your views on school uniform*, I now wonder about the staff. Can the Head insist that I wear a tie? Is not the fact that female teachers are allowed much greater freedom in their choice of attire a breach of the Equal Opportunities Act?

A. Any employer is entitled to make reasonable rules with regard to the dress of his employees and, provided that such

---

*See Chapter 14

rules are generally known, the employer may insist upon compliance.

The main grounds for challenging such a rule would be that it was unreasonable. Were such a challenge to come to court, a judge would take into account whether the rule was published and generally acknowledged and whether it seemed reasonable in the light of the custom and practice prevalent in that and similar workplaces. In the case of teachers, I suspect that a court might very well hold that a governing body was not being unreasonable in setting certain standards of formality and smartness of dress and that, for men, the social convention of wearing a tie is an index of that formality.

Whether the Equal Opportunities Act can be invoked here is doubtful. It would not be seen as reasonable for women to be required to wear exactly the same style of dress as men, because the social convention is quite different. Furthermore, it is much less easy, with feminine attire, to establish where the line is drawn between formality and informality. It was established, for instance, quite some time ago that trousers could be construed as formal wear for women, a judgement which is supported under the Equal Opportunities Act. In the end, the only way to establish the position on ties would be to bring the issue to court. Unless and until you do, the writ of your Head must run.

There are some Heads who have tried to pretend that the limit of 1265 hours does not exist. With out-of-school activities being high on the list of attractions which are thought to make up a 'good' school, this is not altogether surprising. Many teachers contribute a tremendous amount on a voluntary basis, but woe betide the Head who thinks he or she can command it.

Q. The Head of Boys' PE at this school is refusing to undertake any supervision of school teams or run practice sessions for them. What sanctions can we as governors use against him?

A. Probably none. Taking games sessions outside school hours has long been a custom in schools and many teachers, especially PE staff, have given much of their time to such activities. Indeed, it was often thought to be virtually an unwritten aspect of the job of PE teachers that they did this.

The introduction of the *School Teachers' Pay and Conditions of Service Document* in 1987 changed all that by creating the concept of 'directed time', that is, the 1265 hours spread over 195 days during which a teacher is required to work under the reasonable direction of the Head. In addition to teaching and other duties during the school day, Heads have used this time to direct attendance at parents' evenings, staff meetings and other school-related activities.

Generally speaking, Heads have not made use of directed time to cover extracurricular activities, such as school games, plays and concerts, partly because they have continued to regard them as being entirely voluntary and partly because the sheer amount of such activity could not easily be covered by the 1265 hours.

There are exceptions where some of these activities have been directed and, if your school is one, then the teacher concerned is in breach of his contract if he is failing to do what the Head is directing him to do. His only defence would be that the direction itself was unreasonable and this could be tested through the grievance procedure, or, if the Head took disciplinary action against him, through an appeal against it.

There is a reverse side to this argument of which governors should be aware. No activity should be written into a job description, unless it is expected that time will be directed for its performance. Thus, if it were a requirement of the job of Head of Boys' PE that he should coach and supervise certain teams, he would be entitled to expect that time should be allocated for those duties.

Q. Our Head puts pressure on staff to attend functions, such as prize-givings, which are not part of directed time but which he says he hopes staff would wish to attend. What do you advise?

A. Frankly, I don't think your Head is being very fair. If he believes, as well he might, that a particular function is such an important event that teachers ought to be there, he should make no bones about declaring it a part of directed time. If he feels that attendance is genuinely optional, he can issue an invitation, but make it clear that he is not requiring attendance. There is no virtue in fudging directed time requirements: it so often leads to misunderstanding and ill-feeling.

Not all activities outside teaching time are voluntary. Heads will require attendance at staff meetings, parents' evenings and the like. Provided that the total time allocated does not exceed 1265 hours, this is taken to be part of the job.

Q. My Head of Department tells me I must attend a meeting which she has arranged, because it is part of directed time. Surely, only the Head can determine directed time and this cannot be delegated to middle management?

A. It is not uncommon for Heads to allocate a certain amount of directed time for departmental and other group meetings and not unreasonable of them to leave it to the discretion of those responsible for convening those meetings to arrange the details of time and place. They should, however, require certain conditions to be observed, such as good advance notice of dates and times and control over the duration of meetings.

Such delegation is allowed for in the statement of the duties of a Headteacher contained in the *School Teachers' Pay and Conditions of Service Document*, although it is the Head's responsibility to ensure that any direction given to staff is reasonable.

Q. A senior member of my staff has adopted the habit of leaving full staff and other management meetings before the end, on the grounds that she has young children to look after. As these meetings are designated as 'directed time', what should I do about this?

A. The programme of meetings which are included in directed time should be drawn up well in advance and publicized to all staff concerned so that there can be no doubt about what is expected and when.

Once that has been done, you are entitled to expect that all staff required to attend are present for the whole of the meeting, unless they have been excused by you. If the meeting runs over the designated time, then it may be reasonable for someone with another engagement to leave.

Any teacher who feels that the direction of time is unreasonable has the right to take issue with the Head by means of the grievance procedure. Otherwise, failure to accept the direction is a breach of contractual obligation which may be subject to disciplinary action, in this case by a warning not to repeat the offence.

Many teachers have domestic problems which demand their attention in different ways and a sensible Head will always wish to make allowances for emergencies or unusual circumstances. Normally, however, it is the responsibility of the teacher to organize domestic commitments in such a way as not to interfere with professional duties.

So, how does a Head determine what is directed time and what is not?

Q. A teacher on my staff has demanded that I give her a 'time budget'. What exactly does she mean and must I accede to her demand?

A. The concept of the time budget originated in 1987, when Kenneth Baker abolished the Burnham Committee and introduced a new *School Teachers' Pay and Conditions of Service Document*. It was devised by the Secondary Heads Association and was widely adopted as a convenient way to address the innovation of the requirement that a teacher should be available for work under the direction of the Head for up to 1265 hours per annum.

The suggestion was that the Head, in consultation with staff, should draw up a schedule for each member of the teaching staff showing how the hours would be used throughout the year. The timetable of lessons and other pupil time obviously accounted for the great bulk of the time, but specific figures were added for attendance at staff meetings, parents' evenings and at any other events outside normal school hours which the Head deemed to be required rather than voluntary.

The total figures varied from teacher to teacher. A head of a large department might have a higher commitment than a probationer, but calculations showed that it was quite possible to plan for the normal working of the school and still leave each teacher with a balance of hours short of 1265, which could be regarded as contingency time which the Head could take up if the need arose.

Implementing this scheme led many schools to improve the quality of their calendar planning and teachers generally were pleased to have a statement of what was expected of them well in advance. The exercise having been done, the issue of time counting, which many had predicted would become a serious problem, largely disappeared.

It would be going too far, perhaps, to say that your teacher has a *right* to a time budget, but it is an entirely reasonable request to which a sympathetic school management should respond positively.

Of course, what teachers do outside directed time is entirely their own affair, provided that it does not bring their school into disrepute or interfere with the performance of their professional duties.

Q. I read with interest an article about teachers taking a nighttime job boarding up windows. Is the taking on of any job, such as youth work for instance, a breach of one's contract as a full-time teacher?

A. There is nothing to prevent a full-time teacher undertaking any other paid employment outside normal working hours, provided that it does not interfere or conflict with the work which is required under the main contract. Many teachers do, in fact, take on additional work in youth clubs, evening classes and even, so I have heard, pulling pints at the local pub. I make no comment about the desirability or otherwise of this, or about a salary structure which may oblige some teachers to do it, although I suspect that there will always be some who like to add to their income in this way, whatever the circumstances.

Q. One of the teachers at this school has, unbeknown to the Head, been conducting private tuition on school premises. What should be done about this?

A. Assuming that this private tuition is paid for, rather than simply a goodwill provision by the teacher for a struggling pupil, it should be stopped.

No teacher should accept payment for tuition during normal school hours, because this would mean that he or she was accepting a separate contract during the time when he or she was contracted to be working for his or her employer. Outside school hours, a teacher may undertake paid employment of any kind, provided that it does not interfere with contractual obligations to the principal employer. Such private work could only occur on school premises with the permission of the governing body, which could make a charge for the use of its facilities.

It is relevant to observe that the fact that the school premises are being used may convey to the pupil's parents that the tuition is being provided, if not by the school itself, at least with its blessing and approval. This may well not be the case.

It is the responsibility of the Head to see the teacher concerned and to require that the private tuition should be properly separated from the school and conducted in such a way that there is no ambiguity in the minds of any of those concerned.

There is one activity for which a teacher can be paid separately for work done in school and during the school day: lunch-time supervision. Even that creates problems.

Q. Is it possible to pay teachers who undertake midday supervision cash in lieu of a free school meal?

A. It may be possible, but it may not, in practice, prove to be very helpful. Teachers may be engaged as midday supervisors on a separate contract and paid accordingly, the pay including an element reflecting the notional cost of a meal. Such payment is, of course, subject to tax. Given recent decisions on taxable benefits, tax inspectors might even consider a free meal to be taxable, and they certainly would regard a cash payment in that light.

When it comes to the long-suffering Heads and Deputies, however, the lunch-time situation is, to say the least, far from clear.

Q. Can a Head or Deputy undertake paid lunch-time supervision?

A. There are differences of opinion on this question: some LEAs allow it, others say that it is illegal. As it has never been tested in a court, one can only look at the merits of the case.

The Head has the duty to take appropriate measures to ensure the health, safety and good order of pupils throughout the school day, including the midday break. This does not mean that the Head has to be present, or on duty, throughout that time, but simply that he or she must be satisfied that the arrangements are satisfactory and in place. If the Head is not on the premises, a Deputy, or some other competent person, must be left in charge.

It could be argued that a person who is in charge of the premises could not properly fulfil that function, or respond to an emergency situation, if he or she is contractually tied to a specific task in a specific location, which is likely to be the case with paid lunch-time supervision. It would follow logically from this view that a Head could not accept such an appointment, because it would be doing two jobs at once.

However, it could also be argued that the Head, having made arrangements to place a Deputy in overall charge of the premises during the lunch period, could then take on the supervisor's role, knowing that the Deputy would deal with all contingencies. It is clear from this that the Head and Deputies could not all take on supervision at the same time.

A quite different approach could be to argue that Heads and Deputies are not limited by the concept of 'directed time', as applied to all other teachers. On this basis, it may be advanced that the midday break is contractually outside directed time, which leaves teachers free to accept separate contracts for other functions. Heads and Deputies, being outside that provision, might be debarred from accepting separate contracts, even though they are as much entitled to a reasonable break in the middle of the day as anyone else.

The best advice I can offer is to adhere to the old motto: 'If it works, don't fix it'.

Of course, the one place the staff are free to do what they like is their own staffroom. Or is it?

Q. Our LEA is proposing to issue a directive prohibiting smoking in all educational establishments. Do they have the power to do this?

A. In the Articles of Government of schools maintained by LEAs, there is a clause which states that the governing body and the headteacher shall comply with any direction issued to them by the Education Committee concerning health and safety at the school. It seems likely that your LEA is planning to act under the power conferred by this clause.

This presupposes that smoking is a health and safety issue and I doubt whether there are many people nowadays who would argue very seriously that it is not. In any event, there is an Industrial Tribunal decision on the record which indicates that smoking may be considered a health hazard within the meaning of the Health and Safety at Work Act 1974 and thus a matter on which an employer has a duty to act for the protection of all employees.

It would, however, be considered good practice for an employer to consult fully with employees before introducing a ban and to examine alternative courses of action, for example the designation of defined smoking areas.

Even within directed time, the Head's writ is not absolute. One important area in which the teacher is free to choose is religion.

Q. There is some disquiet amongst the staff at this school because, while some teachers regularly attend assemblies, others just as regularly take the opportunity to have a coffee and a chat in the staffroom. Is it not reasonable to expect all teachers to take a fair share of supervising the behaviour of the pupils in assemblies?

A   It may, or it may not, be reasonable, from a personal point of view, to expect teachers to do this, but, if the assembly consists of an act of worship, no teacher can be required to attend.

Section 30 of the Education Act 1944 states the position slightly obliquely but none the less clearly:

> *'Subject as hereinafter provided, no person shall be disqualified by reason of his religious opinions, or of his attending or omitting to attend religious worship, from being a teacher in a county school or in any voluntary school, or from being otherwise employed for the purposes of such a school; and no teacher in any such school shall be required to give religious instruction or receive any less emolument or be deprived of, or disqualified for, any promotion or other advantage by reason of the fact that he does or does not give*

religious instruction or by reason of his religious opinions or
of his attending or omitting to attend religious worship.'

A Head can, of course, require any teacher to attend an assembly for secular purposes, or that part of an assembly which is not an act of worship. Those teachers who decide not to attend the act of worship remain under the direction of the Head during that time and could be given other duties to perform, which would balance the supervisory work which is being undertaken by their colleagues.

Naturally, every teacher expects to have breaks from work during the day, but only one, at midday, is laid down in the Document.

Q. In this church school, all teaching staff are required to attend daily morning assembly. There is no non-contact time, nor an afternoon break. As a result, once a week, each member of staff works from 9 a.m. until lunch-time without a break. If there are absentees, there will be more days without a break. The headteacher is adamant that attendance at assembly is compulsory. Do you consider this to be a fair arrangement?

A. Whether it is fair or not, this arrangement does not infringe the *School Teachers' Pay and Conditions of Service Document*, which specifies only that there should be a break of reasonable length in the middle of the school day.

Unless each teacher has the requirement to attend included in a contract of service or letter of appointment, the headteacher cannot compel attendance at an act of worship, although he or she can direct staff to attend a secular assembly.

Many teachers would argue that a short break for refreshment mid-morning is a useful opportunity to recharge one's batteries, but the need for break-time supervision is bound to mean that those teachers whose turn it is to do that duty may well find themselves in contact with pupils throughout the morning. The smaller the school, the more frequently this duty is likely to come round. I do not believe that your headteacher is being more or less fair in this matter than thousands of other Heads all over the country.

2
Managing the staff

Whenever two or three Heads are gathered together, you can be fairly sure that it will not be long before one of them gets round to saying that any fool can manage the pupils, it's the staff that cause all the problems. Like all old chestnuts, its survival indicates its fundamental truth.

Certainly, personnel management is a vital aspect of the role of Heads and Deputies and a lack of skill in that area can be both disruptive and damaging in even the best of schools. Happily, the great majority of teachers and support staff are dedicated professional people, who give freely of their time and energy and pay little heed to the niceties of employment law or the details of contracts. The minority, on the other hand, can make life very difficult and, being well educated and articulate, they can also be ingenious, persistent and subversive. Not surprisingly, it is the minority whose activities provoke letters to the 'Helpline'.

Before 1987, the teacher's job was not defined and there were frequent arguments about what a Head could legitimately demand. This lack of definition was exploited by some teachers' unions in the 1980s, when they took industrial action by withdrawing from activities which, they claimed, were non-contractual and by making claims about the number of hours for which they were required to work. The inevitable result was a definition of hours and duties, imposed by legislation in 1987 and incorporated annually in the *School Teachers' Pay and Conditions of Service Document*.

Although the Document resolved many contentious issues, it gave fresh scope to the staffroom lawyers to test the limits of the new definitions. Many of the problems are, however, more the result of personal problems and conflicts than of challenges to the law.

Q. Because of a bitter personal disagreement, one of our teachers is refusing to work with a colleague. Their respective duties make it essential that they should cooperate. What can the Head do?

A. Metaphorically speaking, he or she could, and should, bang heads together.

I am assuming that the attempts at mediation which would characterize any civilized community have been tried and failed. It has to be made absolutely clear to this teacher that the Conditions of Service of Teachers makes cooperation and collaboration with the Head and fellow teachers a duty and this duty must come before personal likes and dislikes.

The Head should, therefore, advise this teacher that the refusal to work with any colleague with whom it is necessary that he or she should work is unacceptable and, if persisted with, could lead to disciplinary action. Personal quarrels must be kept apart from professional responsibilities.

Q. An older member of the department I head is openly critical of my decisions and leadership. What can I do about such insubordination?

A. For a start, you can assert your authority by inviting your colleague to meet you privately with a view to resolving the differences between you. It may well be that this teacher, being older and perhaps with longer experience, feels undervalued or ignored and a frank exchange might serve to clear the air and lead to a more cooperative relationship in the future.

If you have introduced regular appraisal into your school, this problem may well be one of the many which will be more readily resolved by using this process. You are likely to be responsible for appraising your colleague and the exercise will provide a natural opening for a discussion of the need for cooperation and support on both sides. An improvement in that area might well be one of this teacher's targets for the following year.

If diplomacy fails, however, you will have to make it clear that open criticism of your actions is both unacceptable and unprofessional. If a warning of that sort is equally ineffective, you may eventually have to refer the matter to your Head, who has the ultimate responsibility for staff discipline.

According to the *School Teachers' Pay and Conditions of Service Document,* a teacher is employed to work 'under the reasonable direction' of the Head. But what is reasonable?

Q. The Head of Art in this secondary school refuses to display pupils' work around the school, unless he is paid an allowance for doing so. He does display work in the Art room, but argues that other Heads of Department are not required to do this. Can I insist and what do I do when he refuses?

A. I have sympathy with your Head of Art on one point. Although Art lends itself to display more than any other subject, I believe that all departments should be encouraged to show their best work in this way and that this should be seen as a whole-school policy to which everyone is expected to contribute.

I have little sympathy with him for the rest of his argument. Displaying pupils' work should be seen as a part of a teacher's duties which should not attract an additional allowance. Your request that he should do it could be converted into a direction and, if he does not wish to accept that, he has recourse to the grievance procedure, where he could argue that you are acting unreasonably. If he loses that, he will have to comply or face disciplinary action.

I am bound to say, however, that I would not recommend that route. It may be better to tackle this by instituting a review of school policy on display, involving all departments. From this might emerge a consensus in which everyone participates and maybe even a coordinator, who may not necessarily be the Head of Art. The Head of Art would be in real difficulty in refusing to join in what everyone else is willing to do.

Q. We wish to direct teachers to visit pupils on work experience at their place of work, as part of our support for those pupils and as a training exercise for the teachers. Is this something which they can refuse to do?

A. There is nothing to stop anyone refusing to do something: the question is whether such a refusal would be reasonable. I do not believe that it would be.

In the statement of a teacher's duties in the *School Teachers' Pay and Conditions of Service Document*, it says, in Section 36 (1)(b), that 'a teacher shall be available to perform such duties at such times and such places as may be specified by the head teacher', and that would seem to cover precisely the point which you raise.

The only grounds for refusal which could be advanced against that would be that the instruction in the particular case was unreasonable, which might be related to the time, the place, the distance to be travelled, the lack of transport or whatever. If a teacher wished to maintain such an argument, the proper channel for doing so would be through the grievance procedure, where the matter could be determined in the prescribed manner.

Q. My Head has instructed me to admit and teach eight three- and four-year-old children in my Reception/Year 1 class on two afternoons a week. The children are not officially admitted to the school until September. Do I have to accept this?

A. I have to say that I am very surprised indeed that your Head should take a step like this without consulting you first and I can see that this creates real difficulties for you.

It is not uncommon for informal arrangements like this to be made these days, but the first duty of the school is to ensure the proper education of the pupils who are legally entitled to it. Teachers are, as I have said many times in this column, required to work under the reasonable direction of the Head. On the face of it, this looks pretty unreasonable and your remedy, if informal discussion does not work, lies in lodging a grievance. If you belong to a union, I recommend that you consult them first.

Q. Our Head has decided to hold some staff meetings at the beginning of the day, 40 minutes before school starts. Have we the right to refuse to attend?

A. In a free country, you can refuse to do anything, but there may be unwelcome consequences. In principle, there is no difference between arranging meetings before school or after, so long as they are using directed time. The only grounds for refusal would be, therefore, that the arrangement was unreasonable.

The argument might be based either upon the fact that it was an unacceptable change to long-standing custom and practice in the school, which seriously affected domestic arrangements, or that it increased the burden upon teachers by having to sit through a meeting before they commenced their principal work of the day. The governing body which heard the grievance would have to judge the case on its merits.

In management terms, one would not expect a Head to introduce a major change of this sort without full consultation with staff and the willing support of most of them.

Q. We have an RE teacher who is refusing to teach RE, arguing that the syllabus she is obliged to follow is unacceptable to her. She cites the 1944 Education Act that no teacher can be obliged to teach religious education. Is there anything that we can do?

A. While it is true that no teacher can be made to teach RE, I do not believe that it is open to a teacher, who has entered into a contract to do so, unilaterally to withdraw from that contract.

I am assuming that this teacher was appointed to teach the subject and has not simply accepted the assignment on a casual basis. In the latter situation, you might have some difficulty in insisting that she continue with it.

While teachers often have the opportunity to discuss the syllabus which has to be followed and may well have flexibility within it, no teacher, whether of RE or of any other subject, has an untrammelled right to determine what will or will not be taught. As this is RE, I imagine that you are referring to an Agreed Syllabus, which has, perhaps, been revised in a way not to this teacher's liking. If she is contracted to teach RE, she has two options: get on with it or get out.

Q. A member of my staff has had a very bad record of attendance over the past year and I have therefore decided not to timetable him for any class preparing for public examination this year. Can this decision be challenged?

A. The allocation of teachers to classes is a key part of the internal management and control of the school and, as such, is part of the Head's statutory duties. In a more general sense, a Head's first obligation is the education of pupils and attaching priority to achievement in public examinations is entirely reasonable in that context.

When a teacher has a poor attendance record, for whatever reason, it is always going to present problems and a Head has to use professional judgement in deciding the appropriate response.

This decision, like every other, is open to challenge through the grievance procedure. A teacher is required to work 'under the reasonable direction' of the Head and, provided that no other aspect of a teacher's conditions of service is breached, a teacher can only argue that the timetable direction which has been given is unreasonable. It would be an unusual governing body which, faced with firm evidence of the kind you describe, would find for the teacher in this situation.

Refusing to do what they should do is one thing. Doing the wrong thing, or doing it badly, is something else.

Q. A parent has alleged that a teacher has struck his son and he is threatening to report the matter to the police. As Head, how should I react?

A. Your reaction should be calm, positive and firm. The fact that this parent is making the threat of telling the police before actually doing so is probably an indication that he wishes you to deal with the matter, while reserving his right to go to law, if your action does not satisfy him.

Even so, you must avoid over-reacting in your efforts to meet his demands. The first step must be to buy time. Tell the parent that you can only deal with the matter if he is ready to leave it with you, at least until you have reported back to him. Promise that the allegation will be thoroughly investigated and that you will report back as soon as possible on your conclusions and consequent actions, but make no other commitment at this stage.

Instruct a Deputy, or other senior member of staff, to conduct the investigation, interviewing both teacher and pupil. Any evidence alleged as physical signs of the assault should be noted and, if possible, examined by a doctor. The teacher should be advised to contact his or her union and invited to make a statement about the incident. Other witnesses, including pupils, should be questioned as quickly as possible, in order to avoid collusion.

When you have the report, you will have to decide what action to take, in the light of the evidence. If you believe that the teacher is guiltless, you must say so and be ready to face the parent, confident that, if he carries out his earlier threat, the police will reach the same conclusion as you did. If you find that the teacher acted improperly, you have to determine the appropriate disciplinary action, in the light of the seriousness of the offence and the teacher's previous record. This may, or may not, need to be taken to a disciplinary committee of the governors, depending on the requirements of the procedure operating in your school. The teacher has a right to appeal against the decision.

None of this deprives the parent of the right to press charges, if he so wishes, but your properly documented investigation will be helpful to the police if necessary.

Q. One of my staff is alleged to have sworn at pupils on several occasions. What should a Head do in such circumstances?

A. That does rather depend on the circumstances. Obviously, if the allegations are true, this teacher is guilty of misconduct. The first step is to investigate the facts and then to take action appropriate to the gravity of the offence. If the offence is mild and the language not extreme, an informal word of advice may be all that is needed. If it is serious, it may be necessary to give the teacher an oral warning that a repetition of the misconduct could lead to further disciplinary action.

It is an interesting fact that pupils of all ages are very upset when teachers use what they consider bad language, even when they may themselves employ far worse in the playground five minutes later or experience it regularly outside the school. This very fact underlines the importance of insisting on the highest professional standards in such matters.

There may be other lessons to be learned from this incident. If the teacher concerned is acting out of character, you may be dealing indirectly with someone who is, for whatever reason, suffering from stress either in work or in private life. While this will not condone the unprofessional behaviour, it may alert you to the need to provide appropriate support or assistance.

It is not only teachers who can get into trouble.

Q. We have a young caretaker who, while being quite good at his job, is causing concern because he is too close to the pupils. He has upset some girls by his remarks and has shared his cigarettes with others. What should the Head do about him?

A. The short answer is that, if he does not desist entirely from the unacceptable conduct after a clear written warning, he should be sacked.

It is a clear condition of employment, written or not, of any employee in a school that a proper adult–child relationship should always be maintained. It may be that the relative youth and inexperience of this young man mean that he has a less than perfect understanding of his position but, once it has been made clear, no further transgression should be accepted.

There is also the little matter of how teachers present themselves for work.

Q. A new teacher has appeared at this school, wearing a nose-stud. Does the head have the right to order its removal and what can be done in the event of a refusal?

A. The case you present should be fairly clear-cut in most schools. The governors would be within their rights to specify that facial adornments, other than earrings, were inappropriate and to instruct the teacher concerned to conform.

Before they do so, however, they should be certain in their minds that they are ready to see the matter through in the event of a refusal. In such a situation, their only recourse would be to suspend the teacher from duty and, ultimately, if the defiance is sustained, dismissal. The teacher would, of course, have the right to challenge this decision at an Industrial Tribunal, although, given that the governing body had acted on a clearly stated and consistent policy, it is hard to believe that a Tribunal would find against them.

Q. Does anyone have the right to set standards for staff dress in a school and can such rules be enforced?

A. All employers have the right to set reasonable standards of personal appearance for their employees and to take disciplinary action against those who deliberately flout them. Schools are no exception and the duties of the employer are exercised by the governing body. It is good practice to have a general policy statement, in order to avoid making hasty judgements when specific cases arise. In drawing up their policy, employers should be careful to avoid statements which might be seen to imply sex or racial discrimination.

Many governing bodies would take the view that a good standard of personal appearance set by the staff plays an important part in establishing similar standards amongst the pupils and so contributes to the ethos of the school. They may therefore, for example, stipulate that leisure wear is not appropriate for work, that protective clothing should be worn in laboratories and workshops and that general appearance should conform to accepted levels of smartness.

A teacher who objects to the standards set, or to their interpretation in practice, has the grievance procedure as a remedy, if discussion reaches an impasse. The onus is on the objector to show that the requirement is unreasonable.

Conduct outside the school may also come under the Head's scrutiny:

Q. Does the fact that a teacher has been declared bankrupt as a result of serious mismanagement of his affairs justify his dismissal from the school?

A. It is not possible to give a straight answer to your question, because that is not exactly the question which the governing body would have to address, if it were minded to consider the matter.

What the governors have to consider – and this is true of any untoward conduct by an employee – is whether the behaviour or action about which complaint is made is such as to render that person unsuitable for employment in the particular job which he or she holds. In taking a view of the matter, the governors would have to consider whether the action or conduct was such as to make that person unsuitable to take charge of pupils or whether it was of such a disreputable nature as to damage the good name of the school.

I suspect that bankruptcy by itself would not constitute sufficient grounds for dismissal, but, if it had arisen as a result of mismanagement or fraud which had become a public scandal, then it might well do so.

It is sometimes helpful to look at the merits of the case from the other end. If the teacher were to be dismissed and if a case for unfair dismissal were taken to an Industrial Tribunal, would the governors be able to demonstrate that they had sound reasons for their decision? Such reasons would have to be founded on evidence as well as on their opinion.

Q. I have received reports that one of my staff is meeting under-age pupils in a public house at the weekend and has purchased alcoholic drinks for them. Do I have any jurisdiction in this matter? If I have, what is the appropriate course of action?

A. I believe that you do have the right to act in this case – and so, too, has the pub landlord, who is being less than vigilant in his stewardship.

The governing body, as the actual or effective employer, has the right to consider any conduct of a teacher which they believe affects the execution of his or her professional duties. It follows, therefore, that, if they have evidence that a teacher is breaking the law and is establishing a relationship with pupils which undermines what they consider to be appropriate as between teacher and pupil, they may consider disciplinary action.

Given that hard evidence exists to support the reports you have received, you should speak to this teacher about the matter and, if it seems serious enough, you may give an oral warning that the conduct is unacceptable and, if continued, could lead to further action. If the teacher feels that this is unjust, the right of appeal to the governing body will provide an opportunity for that to be tested.

Matters of minor indiscipline and appearance can be annoying, but some transgressions need to be taken very seriously indeed.

Q. It has been alleged that one of the teachers at this school has altered examination marks in the course of moderation in order to enhance the results of her own candidates. What is the appropriate action for the Head to take?

A. If true, this is a serious offence which strikes at the very heart of the professionalism of teachers.

If the Head finds that there is at least a case to answer, the teacher should be suspended from duty on full pay while the matter is thoroughly investigated. The examination board should be informed at once so that they can take the measures necessary to protect the integrity of the examination and determine what should be done to protect the interests of the pupils.

If the investigation reveals that the alleged offence was indeed committed, this teacher should be brought before the disciplinary committee of the governing body with a view to dismissal.

It may be necessary for reassurance to be given to the pupils and parents concerned that they have not suffered as a consequence of this regrettable incident.

Q. I was dismissed in 1993 for gross misconduct for helping students to frame answers to questions in a GCSE examination. At the hearing of my case, the Head, who had investigated the case, recommended dismissal. Should he act as prosecutor, judge and jury? An Industrial Tribunal said that I was not unfairly dismissed, although they did not believe that I had encouraged the children to cheat. The LEA reported me to the Department for Education, but they have not removed my licence to teach. Have I been treated fairly?

A. I would not dream of setting my judgement, based on the barest minimum of information, against the authorities you have quoted. In any case, if the facts are as you have stated, you were indeed guilty of gross professional misconduct and the Head was entirely right to recommend dismissal as the appropriate punishment.

He was not acting as judge or jury: that function was fulfilled by the disciplinary committee and, assuming there was one, by the appeal committee. Whether you encouraged the pupils to cheat is irrelevant: you clearly gave them an unfair advantage over other candidates and corrupted the examination process. You are fortunate that the DFE has decided not to debar you from teaching, but it would not surprise me if the examination board insisted that you should not be allowed in future to present candidates for their examinations.

You are obviously having difficulty coming to terms with the seriousness and the foolishness of your conduct. You should understand that teaching is a profession with high ethical standards. You have undermined the trust that pupils, parents and the public place in all teachers and you have paid the proper penalty.

Q. I have reason to believe that a member of my staff has established a close relationship with a sixth-form student. What action, if any, should I take?

A. It has always been a basic tenet of the teaching profession that an intimate relationship between a teacher and a pupil is a breach of professional trust and cannot be tolerated. In higher education, where both parties are adults, many institutions lay down rules of conduct which must be followed when such relationships occur. In schools, no such latitude exists and, in my view, nor should it. Where pupils or students at school or college are involved, it cannot be a relationship between equals and the teacher concerned is abusing his or her position.

I assume from your question that you have at least *prima facie* evidence that this relationship exists. Your first duty, therefore, is to investigate the matter, if necessary suspending the teacher while doing so. If the investigation reveals that the allegation is likely to be true, the matter should be reported to a disciplinary committee of the governors, with the expectation that the outcome will be dismissal.

There are some areas of conduct, however, that should remain private.

Q. As Head, I have received an anonymous letter which makes allegations about the behaviour of one of my staff who, it is claimed, is having an affair with a colleague. What should I do about this? Should I show it to the teacher concerned?

A. Unless one is convinced that an allegation is so serious and so credible that pupils would be put at risk by ignoring it, the best thing to do with anonymous letters is to throw them away.

In this case, you have insufficient grounds even to mount an investigation. Even if the allegation were to be true, there is no reason to suppose that the private conduct of two members of your staff has any bearing upon their professional work and, unless and until you are persuaded otherwise by real evidence, it is, frankly, none of your business.

If the anonymous person who sent the letter has a genuine complaint, he or she should come out into the open and make it in a proper way. The fact of anonymity suggests personal malice and mischief-making and it is no part of your responsibilities to allow yourself to be made use of in this way.

It is helpful, in many instances, if there is a code of conduct in place, which makes clear to all employees the standards which are expected of them.

Q. Should a code of conduct for staff include stipulations concerning their activities outside the school context?

A. Governors of church schools may be particularly inclined in this direction, but, in general, it is ill-advised. It would be reasonable for them to require that teachers did not behave in a manner which would bring the school into disrepute.

The absence of such a stipulation, or indeed of a code of conduct of any description, would not, however, necessarily protect a teacher from disciplinary action. An employer has a general right to protect the integrity of his business against behaviour by an employee which would undermine it.

Misconduct is not the only problem. Unpunctuality and chronic absenteeism create difficulties for schools and colleges, just as they do in other walks of life.

Q. A teacher at this school has been seen cycling around the village, although he has been absent, certified ill by his doctor. Do we have a case for disciplinary action?

A. I doubt it. The fact that a doctor has signed a certificate to say that someone is unfit to work does not necessarily mean that the patient is confined to his home. For all you know, the doctor might have given the classical medical advice to get plenty of exercise and fresh air, which is precisely what this teacher seems to be getting.

If you have more substantial reasons for believing that this teacher is malingering, the employer may request a separate medical examination in order to have a second opinion.

As far as disciplinary action is concerned, you should be aware that there is a case on record of a man who claimed that he was unfairly dismissed, when he had been seen by his employer on the golf-course while officially off sick. He won.

Q. We have a teacher who is frequently late and often absent for odd days or half-days for reasons which are usually related to the need to care for her child, who, to judge by the number of medical appointments, does not enjoy the best of health. Her colleagues are as fed up with covering for her as I am. What can be done?

A. This is one of those cases which can only be resolved by examining one's priorities. The school has a prime duty to its pupils and a teacher who is too often absent is depriving her pupils of their entitlement. However sorry one may feel for her domestic difficulties, the needs of the pupils must come first.

A teacher who has domestic problems has to accept that it is her responsibility to ensure that, emergencies apart, arrangements are made to cope with the normal care of her child which do not interfere with her performance of the duties for which she is employed and paid. Given that the situation you describe has been going on for a long period, this teacher must be warned that her record is unacceptable and must be improved. Firm action should not preclude sympathetic support and either you or an appropriate senior colleague may well discuss with her ways in which she can be helped.

Q. Does ill-health constitute reasonable grounds for dismissal?

A. In certain circumstances, it can. A contract of employment is a legally binding arrangement between an employer and an employee whereby the former undertakes to pay the latter in return for services specified or implicit in that contract. The contract may be terminated if either side fails to fulfil his or her obligations. Employment law exists to define more clearly the rights of both sides in relation to such contracts and protects the employee against arbitrary termination by the employer.

Where ill-health or other incapacity prevents the employee from fulfilling the contract over a prolonged period, the employer may consider that the contract has been, as the lawyers say, frustrated and thus, in effect, terminated.

Arrangements for sick-pay, which usually specify reduced pay after a set period of absence and eventually no pay at all, are a recognition of the variation of the contract which is triggered by prolonged absence. Employers would normally be expected to respect these arrangements and not to terminate a contract at least until the no pay position is reached.

Difficulties arise when the absences are frequent but not continuous, a situation which is often more disruptive than long-term illness. Where such absences continue over a very long period, an employer could be justified in terminating the contract and, if the employee claimed unfair dismissal before an Industrial Tribunal, the employer might well be vindicated.

A governing body considering such a situation should take appropriate professional advice before proceeding. In some cases, the alternative of premature retirement on grounds of ill-health may be a more appropriate way of resolving the difficulty for both sides.

Politicians are quick to win public applause by calling for the speedy removal of incompetent and failing teachers. No Head would disagree with them, but they know, often from personal experience, that it is seldom a simple matter.

Q. A teacher of many years of service is now the subject of an investigation by the Head, following complaints from parents about his competence. His lessons have been observed by the Head and others and he has been interviewed by the Head, all without advance notice, other than a general advice, which he accepted, that the investigation would take place. He now feels very stressed. Has the Head acted correctly and reasonably?

A. It is entirely reasonable that a Head should respond to complaints of incompetence, if there is sufficient substance in them to warrant an investigation. It is professionally correct to advise the teacher of the nature of the complaints, to invite comments and to indicate what action is proposed.

What I fear is lacking in this case is a properly established competency procedure which sets out exactly how the matter should be handled and what the rights of the teacher are. Many LEAs and governing bodies rely upon their statements of disciplinary procedure for this purpose, but this is rarely entirely satisfactory or appropriate for the more complex business of competency.

The Head has the right to visit classrooms at any time and, indeed, to interview teachers, but, where a teacher has been advised that an investigation is to take place, it would have been better to have set out in advance what the process of investigation was going to be, over what period of time and when the evaluation of the exercise was to be completed. Such a programme would have been as helpful to the Head as to the teacher, because it would have established a clear beginning and end and a point where some sort of decision would need to be made.

Given such a framework, the Head could then indicate the various aspects of the teacher's performance to be looked at and those might include lesson preparation and presentation, classroom control, marking of books, compliance with administrative requirements and so on. In that context, the teacher could be warned to expect random visits to his classroom and other spot-checks upon his work.

At the conclusion of the exercise, the Head would have to decide whether the complaints were well founded or not. If they were not, no further action would be needed. If they were, it would be necessary to warn the teacher that further action might follow, if improvements in identified areas of performance were not made over a set period, and to put in place appropriate training or support in order to help the teacher achieve the targets.

From the account which has been given, this Head has acted within his or her powers, but has been insufficiently sensitive to the effects of the process on the teacher and insufficiently precise in setting out his or her own plan of action. The outcome may well leave both parties feeling dissatisfied.

Q. As Head, I am conducting a competency exercise on a PE teacher, concentrating on lesson planning and presentation. One of his problems is that he is seriously overweight and unable to participate in many of the activities which he is teaching. Am I entitled to take this into consideration in assessing his competence or would this be deemed unfair, if the process ended in dismissal? Should not a PE teacher set an example of a healthy lifestyle?

A. It is important to distinguish between this teacher's professional competence to teach and his physical capacity to undertake the responsibilities which are a part of the job.

It might well be argued that a disabled person was fully competent as a professional teacher, even of PE, if he had a good command of the subject and the ability to ensure that his pupils received the full benefits of a balanced and well-presented programme. The ability to demonstrate skills may well be an advantage, but it may not be an absolute requirement if a gifted pupil, under guidance, can equally well serve as an example.

The question of physical capacity is a separate consideration. Pupils doing a full range of PE activities may well perform some exercises, for example vaulting in a gymnasium, where the presence of a reasonably agile supervisor is needed to ensure their safety in the event of a mistake or accident. Someone who was physically unable to make that response might be unsuited to that task. The same may apply with some field games and athletics.

If, in your professional judgement, the teacher's physical condition is such as to jeopardize the safety of pupils, you have a duty to remedy the situation, if necessary by terminating the teacher's contract, quite apart from any consideration of his professional competence.

The question of setting an example is difficult to establish, unless you were in a position to produce a document from the school's staff handbook or LEA guidance which specifically indicated this as a requirement. It is hard to establish that a teacher is failing in a duty, if that duty has never been spelt out.

You do not say, except by implication, whether this teacher's condition is the consequence of a physical disorder or simply his own overindulgence. If the former, he should be seeking appropriate medical advice. If the latter, he may need some specialist advice, not perhaps from you, but rather from the LEA Adviser for PE.

One last thought: it is often said that overeating, like anorexia, is a physical manifestation of personal or psychological problems. You are dealing with a teacher whose performance is unsatisfactory. It could be that the stresses of failure over a period of time, now exacerbated by the fact that he is under scrutiny, have something to do with his weight problem. Resolve the one and the other may resolve itself.

Q. We have a long-serving teacher in his late fifties whose level of competence is now seriously questioned and about whom there have been a growing number of complaints from parents.

Suggestions of early retirement have fallen on deaf ears. What should I, as Head, do about it?

A. It is very sad when someone who has no doubt given long and dedicated service in the profession reaches the position which you describe. Nevertheless, however much sympathy you may feel for this teacher, you have to remember that your first duty is to the pupils for whose education you are responsible and who may well be suffering disadvantage because of his failures.

It would be painful for all concerned to embark on competency proceedings at this stage of his career, although this must be the ultimate course if all else fails. Your best hope is to find a way to persuade him to consider again the attractions of early retirement. It will help if your governing body or LEA has a scheme for enhancement in these circumstances but, even if there is not one, many people are unaware of the extent of their pension rights after many years of service.

As Head, you are probably not the best person to try to do the persuading: no matter how kindly the approach, it can be perceived as intimidating when coming from someone in authority. If you have a good local adviser, he or she might be able to make a convincing case, but the best person might be a representative of the union or association to which the teacher belongs. They are often very experienced in handling problems of this sort and they may tip the balance, when they appreciate that what is being proposed is really in the best interests of their member.

Whether as a result of misconduct or of incompetence, some teachers are going to be dealt with through formal procedures. It is very important that everyone concerned has a clear idea of what those procedures are and how they operate. Failure to do things properly has spoiled many a good case.

In the case of serious misconduct, it may be necessary to suspend the person concerned while the investigation of the matter is undertaken.

Q. Our disciplinary procedure says that the suspension of a teacher is 'a neutral act'. Surely the fact that you have been suspended will appear on your record and so count against you? People are bound to believe that 'there is no smoke without fire', aren't they?

A. The procedure statement is quite correct. All procedures provide for the suspension of an employee while allegations of a serious nature are investigated or where the employer has other good *prima facie* reason for suspension. Such a suspension is on full pay and, should the investigation exonerate the employee from any wrongdoing or the particular reason for the suspension cease to operate, the employee may resume duties without any inference to be drawn. There is absolutely no reason why, in such cases, the suspension should be recorded or referred to again, officially or otherwise. Should an employee find that such is not the case, he or she would have a legitimate cause for grievance.

There are occasions when the situation becomes further complicated by the involvement of the Child Protection Agency or the police. This may mean that the school has to suspend its own investigation of the matter, while the outside enquiry is made. This does not mean, however, that the school cannot, in the end, pursue its own disciplinary procedure.

Q. One of our pupils complained to the police that a teacher had physically assaulted her. After investigating the alleged incident, the police decided to take no action and the staff are now saying they will not teach the girl because she has acted maliciously. The investigation did reveal, however, that the teacher had acted improperly, albeit not so badly as was alleged. What should be done?

A. The Head of a school has a duty to deal with misconduct by staff regardless of whether a crime has been committed. This teacher probably deserves at least an oral warning for the incident.

Getting the staff to understand the truth of the matter, without pillorying their colleague, is a little more difficult. I should be inclined to call in the union representatives and to give them a full explanation of what has happened and why. That should be sufficient to ensure that the word goes round that this case is not one for the barricades.

The conduct of any disciplinary procedure should always be meticulously in accordance with the written statement adopted by the governors. Where there is any doubt, considerations of natural justice should always be uppermost and every care should be taken to ensure that the defendant has every opportunity to present his or her side of the case.

Q. Procedures for disciplinary and grievance hearings usually refer to the right of the 'defendant' to be accompanied by a friend. Who can be a friend and can there be more than one?

A. A friend in this context is a long-established legal usage to allow the right of representation in specified circumstances. A friend in such cases can be anyone whom the individual chooses to nominate and may be a total stranger. Commonly, in the teaching profession, the friend will be an official of the trade union to which the teacher belongs, although sometimes a solicitor, or even a barrister, may be selected. It is not the business of the panel hearing the case to interfere with the right of the defendant to nominate whomsoever he or she pleases, provided that it is done in conformity with the procedures as laid down.

A literal interpretation would suggest that the friend is singular and one would certainly not wish to have the proceedings cluttered up with an army of supporters. It would probably be unnecessarily officious, however, to deny the presence of one or two additional advisers, provided that it is clear that only one is the designated friend and the only one to speak.

Q. Is it acceptable for a spouse to appear in the capacity of 'friend'?

A. I believe that it would be most undesirable to allow this to happen. The whole point of having a 'friend' is to have someone who is detached from the situation and who can represent the principal party without the burden of personal and emotional involvement. It is hard to imagine a spouse being able to perform that role effectively and, while there are no rules laid down about it, I think that any adjudicating panel would be justified in saying that such a representation was unacceptable and in allowing an opportunity for a change of mind.

Q. The disciplinary procedure lays down four levels of sanction. How should one decide which is appropriate in any particular case? Can one omit levels?

A. This is always a difficult issue for Heads and governors alike and the application of common sense may well provide a better answer than any preconceived rules.

Clearly, if the offence is of such a nature that the employer cannot contemplate the person concerned resuming normal duties, dismissal is the only possible decision, whether there has been previous disciplinary action or not. Governors should put themselves in the place of parents and consider what their reaction would be to their own child being taught by a person guilty of the offence brought before them.

In other cases, the previous disciplinary record, if any, should be taken into account as well as the seriousness of the offence. It is useful, too, to consider whether the action taken is likely to be effective in preventing a recurrence. Often, the shock of being on the receiving end of a formal process is quite enough to prevent any further problem.

In the end, there are two considerations to be kept in mind. The first, and the most important by far, is the need to ensure that every pupil in the school is well and properly taught. The second is that one is dealing with the livelihood of a trained and skilled person, whose career should not be terminated, unless there is no alternative.

Whatever is decided, there is always the right of appeal and this, too, can create its own problems:

Q. The governing body of this maintained school recently dismissed a teacher for serious misconduct. The appeals committee of the LEA has reinstated the teacher and substituted a final written warning for dismissal. The governors are appalled by this decision and many parents are protesting. What can we do?

A. The short answer is nothing. The whole purpose of having an appeal procedure is to allow for a decision to be reviewed by a separate body, which has had no involvement with the case. If, on every occasion an appeal was made, it was rejected, there would be no point in having it. However perverse some people may think the decision to be, there is no way in which it can be overturned, unless the procedure allows for a further stage or unless it can be demonstrated that the appeals body has proceeded incorrectly or has made a decision which no reasonable person, presented with the facts, could have been expected to take. In the latter case, an application to the High Court for judicial review or an appeal to the Secretary of State that the LEA has acted unreasonably in the exercise of its powers might be possibilities.

From the brief statement you have provided, it seems unlikely that the appeal committee has acted in a way which could be deemed unreasonable in law. It has concurred with the governing body that serious misconduct took place, but has disagreed with the penalty, as it has the right to do if it is so persuaded.

Your governors have no option but to accept the decision with good grace and to inform parents that appropriate disciplinary action has been taken. They can also be assured that, should the offence be repeated, the chances of an appeal being again success-ful would be slight.

It is the duty of the Head to take whatever steps may be neces-sary in the school, either to remove the teacher from the situation where there is a risk of repetition of the offence or to provide an appropriate level of supervision and monitoring both to support the teacher and to prevent a recurrence. The teacher must be left in no doubt as to the seriousness of the position or the conse-quences of further misconduct.

Some forms of misconduct render the teacher concerned unfit to be placed in charge of young people anywhere.

Q. We have just dismissed a teacher for offences which, in our view, make him a menace to children anywhere. What should we do to ensure that he is not employed in a school again?

A. This is not a decision for you to take, however strongly you may feel about the case. The governing body of the school, or the LEA, has a duty to report the facts of the case to the Department for Education and Employment. The Department will review the case and will allow the teacher concerned to make representations to them, if he wishes to do so.

If the department reaches the same conclusion as you have done, the teacher's name will be included in what is known as List 99. This either specifies that the person should not be employed at all in contact with young people or places limits, for example of gender, where employment may be considered. The names of all newly appointed teachers are checked against the list, a copy of which is held by Local Education Authorities.

Q. A teacher at the independent school, of which I am a governor, has recently resigned and I have reason to believe that his departure resulted from an improper relationship with a pupil. Should the facts of this case be reported to the Department of Education and Science?

A. If your belief is correct, this case should have been reported. Under the Education (Particulars of Independent Schools) Regulations 1982 (SI No. 1730), the proprietor of an independent school is obliged to make a report to the Secretary of State concerning any teacher who is dismissed on the grounds of misconduct, or who would have been dismissed, or considered for dismissal, had he not first resigned. The duty to do so is laid upon the proprietor, which in your case I imagine is the board of governors, although one would normally expect the task to be delegated to the Head.

3
Illness and accidents

If no teacher and no member of the support staff were ever ill and if no accidents ever occurred in schools, the task of management would be a great deal easier, but, human nature and random chance being what they are, the management of the consequences of illness and accidents is an inevitable and unpredictable part of school leadership. I refer here not to major disasters or epidemics, which call for special measures and skills, but to the everyday experience of life in any school or college.

This everyday experience can involve those who are employed to work at the institution, those who come there to learn and those who are just visiting. We look first at those who are employed.

For them, and indeed for the other categories too, it is a sad fact of modern life that the common reaction to any accident is to ask whether there is any chance of financial compensation.

Q. One of my staff recently slipped on a polished floor in the school and suffered a painful back injury, necessitating medical treatment and some time off school. Is he, or the school, entitled to any compensation?

A. The teacher concerned should immediately consult his union, if he belongs to one. It is quite possible that a claim for his injuries could be made against the LEA, assuming that the condition of the floor was indeed the cause of the accident and was the responsibility of the LEA. Such a claim would involve loss of earnings, if any, as a result of the injury, which means that, if he was paid normally out of the school budget, there would be no actual loss to the school.

Claims of this sort can lead to prolonged disputes, where the liability is in dispute and an insurance company is reluctant to pay up. Many cases will be settled by agreement, in order to avoid the expense of a costly court battle. Even so, many cases are far from straightforward when it comes to determining liability.

Q. An accident occurred when a cupboard being delivered to the school fell from the van and injured a teacher who was assisting the van driver, who was on his own and unable to handle it by himself. Who was responsible for the injury?

A. It is always the person who is trying to be helpful and get a job done who gets hurt. We all know that the delivery company should have sent sufficient staff to do the job properly and we know also that we should not let pupils get involved. It seemed only sensible to give a helping hand and I do not suppose the teacher concerned gave a second's thought before doing so.

If there is a claim for injury arising from this unfortunate incident, there are a number of choices. If the van driver asked for or accepted the offer of help, the claim might go to the delivery company. If the teacher had acted entirely on his own initiative, the carrier might deny liability and the school or local authority might argue that they have no liability either for what was an act of negligence quite outside what the teacher is expected to do. As it happened on school premises, however, they might well make a payment *ex gratia*, rather than meet the costs of a legal wrangle. Finally, the teacher might find that his union provides cover for injuries sustained in the course of professional duties, though whether unloading vans counts as a professional duty is the sort of question which keeps our learned friends in gainful employment.

The moral of the tale is, I am afraid, that being helpful may not always be the right course of action. It may be better to leave the moving of cupboards to those who are experienced in the business and insured against the concomitant risks.

While employers may take responsibility for what happens to the person, they are unlikely to accept responsibility for personal property.

Q. My car has been damaged in the school car park to the tune of £400 by the accidental consequences of irresponsible behaviour by pupils. Am I entitled to compensation?

A. It is likely that your employer, whether local authority or board of governors, does not take responsibility for your car while it is on school premises, even though you are allowed to bring it and to park it there. They will not, therefore, take responsibility for any damage which takes place, unless the damage was the direct consequence of an action or negligence by them.

Depending on circumstances, some employers are sometimes prepared to make *ex gratia* payments in partial compensation for such damage and some teachers' unions operate schemes to cover such cases. You do have a right to pursue the culprits, if identified, or their parents, for damages, but this may not be fruitful.

If you are comprehensively insured, your only loss may be of a part of a 'no claims' bonus and you may have more success if you confine any other claim to meeting that smaller amount.

There are many activities in schools which may give concern with regard to legislation on Health and Safety and to the duty of care to be exercised in respect of pupils and students. This is particularly true in areas of potential danger, such as Science laboratories, workshops and Home Economics rooms.

Q. As a teacher of Design and Technology, one of my foremost concerns is safety in the workshop. Bearing this in mind, could you clarify the following:

(a) Is there a maximum class size by law that a teacher should be responsible for?

(b) Must the workshop layout be such that all pupils at all times should be visible to the teacher in charge, by law or just good sense?

A. There is no specific statutory law on these matters: they are governed by the common law duty of care and by any regulations which the employer may make.

There is no area where the duty of care needs to be more carefully exercised than in workshops, especially where there are potentially hazardous machines present. The exact number of pupils one might expect to take together in a workshop will depend on many factors, such as the size of the room, the nature of the equipment, the age and nature of the pupils and the work to be undertaken.

The responsibility for determining this number rests with the Head, who must make a professional judgement about it. If a teacher believes that the Head's decision creates an unacceptable hazard, he or she has the duty to say so and, if unable to obtain satisfaction, may have recourse to the grievance procedure, on the grounds that the direction to teach in those conditions is unreasonable. In LEA schools, it may be helpful to seek the advice of a specialist adviser.

Once the pupils are in the workshop, it is the responsibility of the teacher to ensure that they are properly supervised. Here again, the requirements will be determined by the same kind of factors already listed. Clearly, the teacher's eyes cannot be everywhere at once, but the instructions to pupils must be clear and should, as a matter of routine, include emergency procedures. As far as is practicable, the teacher should have good sight lines to potentially hazardous areas and should have good access to emergency switches.

It is important to remember that, should an accident occur, the test by which the situation will be judged will be that of reasonableness: did those responsible exercise the degree of supervision and care which, in all the material circumstances, would be judged to be reasonable? This may not be as cut and dried as you would like, but, given the infinite variety of situations, it is ultimately the best yardstick.

Specialist teachers have both training and experience in working in specialist rooms and are rightly concerned when others, who lack their expertise, are asked to work in them:

Q. Is it acceptable for non-Science teachers to teach in laboratories?

A. Decisions about who teaches whom and where fall within the professional responsibilities of the Head. There are no legal provisions governing this question. The Head's judgement must be based on the nature of the laboratory, an evaluation of the hazards, the number and behavioural standards of the pupils and the competence of the teacher.

Laboratories are potentially hazardous places, more hazardous certainly than the normal classroom. The presence of water and gas taps, additional power points, apparatus and possibly chemicals makes it essential that pupils should be properly supervised. This is not to say that only a trained Science teacher is capable of exercising that supervision satisfactorily, but it does mean that no teacher, scientist or otherwise, should supervise activities of which he or she is not in full control. It also means that any non-Science teacher using the laboratory must observe the rules which the Head of Science lays down for its use.

Some schools are very short of rooms and, as one who taught many a history lesson in laboratories in my time, I know how inconvenient it can be, although I did make good use of their Davy lamp, supported by a demonstration with a Bunsen burner and a piece of gauze.

In one sense, the following query was not about an accident, although the opportunity for what took place may have been created accidentally. It does, however, underline the need to insist on high standards in managing all potentially hazardous situations.

Q. A pupil removed a dangerous substance from the store of our Technology Department. Thanks to prompt action by the police, it was recovered and no harm was done. What action should the Head take to deal with the matter?

A. The first question must be to find out whether the substance was genuinely needed by the department and for what purpose. The second is to establish how it came to be left in a place where it was possible for the pupil to get hold of it. The third is to investigate the misbehaviour of the pupil concerned.

From all these enquiries, disciplinary action may follow. If there was no good reason for the substance to be in the school, the person who brought it there should at least be given a formal warning. If it was needed by the department, the question of the security of this and other dangerous substances should be thoroughly examined with a view to ensuring that such a theft could not happen again. If there was an element of negligence in leaving the substance where the pupil had access to it, the person who was responsible for that neglect may need to be warned also.

The relatively easy part, I suspect, is to discipline the pupil and his or her punishment will, as ever, depend upon the circumstances, the motivation and the degree of remorse for what was, at best, extremely foolish, and, at worst, criminal.

It is sadly true that teachers today are concerned about the hazards they may face in dealing with violent behaviour both from pupils and sometimes from their parents and others. Naturally, they expect to be given reasonable protection from those hazards – but what is reasonable?

Q. Do you think that an LEA might be failing in its duty of care to its employees if a headteacher required teachers to work alone with groups of children who are known to be potentially violent or who are likely to make unfounded allegations of assault? Is it necessary for incidents to occur before the legal situation is clarified?

A. There are many teachers who accept a degree of risk every day in the work which they do with seriously disturbed children. They accept the risk as a part of the job, although they expect their employer to adopt reasonable measures to protect them and to compensate them in the event of injury.

By reasonable measures, I mean safety precautions appropriate to the particular situation: an alarm, someone else within call, other adults present, and so on. It is hard to be specific because every situation carries its own risks and requires its own arrangements.

That is why it is difficult to answer your second question about the law being clarified. Certainly, an employer has a duty of care to an employee in providing reasonable protection from known or perceived dangers inherent in the nature of the work and, if an injured employee could demonstrate that the employer had been negligent in that respect, damages might be awarded. The outcome would, however, turn on the circumstances and upon what a court might deem reasonable in the particular case. No amount of legislation can be helpful in covering the multiplicity of situations which exist.

If an employee feels that he or she is being asked to work in situations where the degree of risk is unreasonable, the issue can be raised both informally and formally through a number of channels, including Health and Safety representatives, grievance procedures and trade union representation. The duty to avoid unnecessary risk is the responsibility of the employee as well as the employer.

The risk of accidents and other untoward events may be increased when pupils are placed in the care of the inexperienced and, with the introduction of school-based teacher training, this question has been given added focus:

Q. Should students on initial teacher training be left alone in charge of classes? What is the legal position?

A. Every student needs to have the self-confidence of 'flying solo' at the appropriate stage and it is part of the responsibility of those supervising training to judge when the time is right to do so. It should be a planned phase in development for which the student has been prepared. The mentor should be available, if needed, and the student should know what to do if help is required.

The legal position is no different from the normal situation. The responsibility of ensuring that the pupils are properly supervised and taught rests ultimately with the Head. In this instance, this is delegated to the mentor, who exercises professional judgement that the student is capable of taking charge of the class, a decision for which the mentor is accountable. The student, who is not an employee, has the duties of any responsible adult placed in charge of young people.

Of all the physical dangers which have been encountered in recent years, and not just in schools, the most alarming has been exposure to asbestos dust. Asbestos was used in the construction of many public buildings, schools and colleges included, and, although most of the problems have now been eliminated, concerns are still raised whenever repair work is undertaken, especially on older buildings.

Q. *Some time ago, the TES featured a disturbing article concerning the dangers of asbestos in schools. Is there any way of finding out whether asbestos is present in a particular school?*

A. When the hazards of asbestos, or certain types of asbestos, became generally known, local education authorities inspected all their buildings and took remedial action where necessary. Since that time, there have been strict controls on its use in building. If you are concerned about a particular school, the relevant department of the LEA should be able to offer you the assurance you need. In the case of an independent school, the governors have the responsibility for the buildings and should be asked to provide evidence that they have eliminated any possible dangers.

There are also less serious health concerns which may affect those who work in schools:

Q. *One of our office staff is complaining about eyestrain as a result of working with a word processor. Does the governing body bear any responsibility in this matter?*

A. Very probably it does. If it can be shown that the condition is directly related to the conditions of work, it comes under the Health and Safety at Work Act and the employer is required to do something about it.

The problem may be remedied by changing the position of the screen or altering the lighting arrangements. Possibly, the individual may need to wear special glasses when working on the word processor. Perhaps the person should be given more varied work, so that shorter periods are spent in front of the screen.

Expert advice should be sought and, whatever is advised, the governing body should, as far as it reasonably can, see that it is provided, including purchasing the glasses, if that is what is prescribed.

From the teacher's point of view, a prime concern is the duty of care for the pupils and, in particular, for the location of responsibility when something goes wrong.

*Q. This school allows pupils to attend courses in motor-cycle train-
ing, where the parents pay the course fees directly to the organizers. As it is promoted by the school, a member of staff accompanies
the pupils. Does the school have any responsibility in the event of
an accident?*

A. If the school is as closely involved as you suggest, parents are
likely to infer that, even though they are paying the course
organizers, the activity is, to some degree, a part of the school's
extra-curricular activities.

I am sure that the organizer is fully covered against possible
liabilities – you should check this and not take it for granted – but
you should also check with your school insurers that they will
cover any liability which might be attached to the school, arising
out of this activity.

It is a particular worry when the pupils do not do as they are told
and the following question makes this point very well:

*Q. We have fitted seat-belts in our school minibus. What are the
legal responsibilities of teachers, whether driving or not, to ensure
that pupils are wearing them at all times?*

A. As so often, we are back to what is reasonable. Where seat-
belts are fitted, they should be worn and pupils should be so
instructed at the start of the journey. A notice to that effect
should be prominently displayed in the vehicle. The teacher in
charge should make a visual check before starting.

Where there is a teacher, or other responsible adult, travelling
as a passenger, it should be easy to ensure that pupils remain
'belted up' throughout the journey. Where the driver is the only
adult, it is impossible to maintain such close supervision, although
a responsible youngster might be told to keep an eye on the
others. Where the teacher in charge has taken reasonable steps to
ensure appropriate safety standards, the law should be satisfied.

Dealing with pupils who have unusual health problems can
present difficulties for schools, who feel much less happy about
accepting responsibility in an age where litigation is becoming so
common. This applies even to such simple matters as administering medicines and the following case illustrates the point:

Q. We have been advised that we have a pupil who is highly allergic to bee-stings, to the extent that an injection is needed very quickly if he is stung. Should the school accept responsibility for administering this?

A. I do not believe that any teacher should accept responsibility for this, because, if anything went wrong, he or she might not escape an action for negligence. Even a signed parental permission would not absolve anyone from such liability. If the condition is so serious that the risk cannot be accepted without the presence of an appropriately trained nurse, then this boy should attend a school where such a facility is available.

My answer elicited a furious response, which allowed me the opportunity to extend and moderate my advice:

Q. Do you realize that, in your answer regarding a child with bee-sting allergy, you are recommending the exclusion of many children from schools? There are hundreds of children with serious food allergies, mostly to peanuts, and almost all carry an adrenalin injection on doctor's advice. In many cases, caring teachers, trained in First Aid, have accepted responsibility for their treatment and some enlightened LEAs have issued indemnity policies. Were you suggesting that these 'normal' children should be sent to special schools?

A. No, I was not, and I do realize that such problems are not uncommon. Many mainstream schools, particularly secondary schools, do have a trained nurse on the premises and can deal with this kind of situation.

Unfortunately, we live in a litigious age and no teachers can be certain that they will not be held liable for acts of commission or omission, if they accept responsibility for medical treatment of pupils. Parents are very willing to trust teachers to undertake procedures which are normally simple and straightforward, but, should something go wrong, their attitude can change dramatically. It is very easy to suggest that there has been a failure to act in time or in the right way. No teacher wishes to be accused of responsibility for the death of a child. Hence my advice.

If a teacher, who has received appropriate training – and this may not necessarily be covered by elementary First Aid courses

– is willing to take on the responsibility, then so be it. It would none the less be wise to do so only on condition that the employer accepts ultimate responsibility and indemnifies that teacher against any consequent liability. As a result of my initial comments, I have received evidence that a number of employers have acted in this way. This is good practice, which should be applied wherever it is needed.

Some teachers have been concerned about AIDS and there have been one or two well-publicized cases:

Q. I have been informed that one of our students is HIV positive. In the absence of an LEA policy covering this situation, what should I do?

A. One cannot repeat too often the fact that, although AIDS is extremely serious, it is virtually impossible to transmit it other than through sexual intercourse or misuse of injections. This student does not represent a threat to staff or other students and there is no need to inform all and sundry of his or her condition.

It would, however, be prudent to inform those members of staff who have pastoral responsibility for this student and those who might find themselves in the situation of dealing with a physical injury, for example PE or workshop staff.

The most common accidents on school premises are, of course, accidents to pupils and every school will have well-established procedures for dealing with them. Here, too, the question of responsibility may arise:

Q. What are a teacher's responsibilities when a pupil is injured or ill and a parent cannot immediately be contacted?

A. The teacher's duty in such circumstances is to deal with the matter as a reasonable parent could be expected to do and the first priority must be the welfare of the pupil.

I assume from your question that you are referring to situations where it is more than a question of allowing the pupil to rest quietly and keep warm until he or she feels better, or can be sent home. Where it appears to the teacher (or, in most circumstances, to the Head or most senior person available) that the condition of the pupil is such as to require urgent medical attention and where reasonable attempts to contact the parents have been unsuccessful, medical assistance should be sought as speedily as possible, if necessary by summoning an ambulance. In the most serious cases, the very first act would be to summon the ambulance. Depending on the circumstances, the school might well wish to allow a responsible adult to accompany the pupil to the hospital.

Once the pupil is in the care of the medical services, the duty of care is passed to them and they, too, will seek to contact the parents. The school would, none the less, wish to maintain its own efforts to ensure that the parents are traced and informed as quickly as possible. Once the parents are informed and in a position to take over their proper responsibility, the responsibility of the school ceases.

Finally, the school should have established procedures to ensure that the facts of the incident and the action taken are duly recorded.

Q. When a pupil has to be taken to hospital by ambulance, does the school have an obligation to send a teacher with him?

A. It is a well-established concept that a school acts *in loco parentis* and, in situations like this, should do exactly what a responsible parent would do.

In practical terms this means that, having made an immediate attempt to contact the parents to ascertain whether they are in a position to take responsibility themselves, the school remains responsible until they do. This responsibility means doing what, in the school's judgement, is in the best interests of the pupil.

In almost every case, this will necessitate ensuring that the pupil is accompanied by a responsible adult – not necessarily a teacher – either until the parents arrive to take over, or until that adult is satisfied that the pupil is in safe care at the hospital.

As in so many things, however, decisions may be affected by the circumstances of the case. It might not, for instance, be thought necessary to send anyone other than a reliable fellow-student with a mature sixth-former with a relatively minor injury.

This answer also provoked an objection:

Q. With reference to your advice about accompanying pupils to hospital, surely it should be acceptable to leave them in the care of the ambulance service, who are trained and competent to deal with traumatic situations? Is there not also a risk that other children may be left without adequate supervision?

A. Yes, of course ambulance service personnel are capable of taking charge of the sick or injured pupil. The point of the accompanying teacher or other adult from the school is first to provide the reassurance to the pupil of a familiar face and second to do what a responsible parent would wish to do in such circumstances.

As always, the decision is a matter of professional judgement on the spot and the needs of other pupils have to be taken into account in making it.

This last answer underlines the fact that schools are very caring institutions, which go out of their way to ensure that their pupils and students receive the best possible personal attention. This last rather unusual case is another example of this, even if they were being a little pernickety about the cost.

Q. One of our GCSE candidates last summer was injured just before the examinations and we had to employ an amanuensis to write his papers for him. Can we pass the cost of this on to the parents?

A. The regulations about charging make it clear that a charge cannot be levied in respect of any tuition, materials or equipment used in preparing a pupil to take a public examination which is offered by the school, nor can the cost of entries for such examinations be passed on. On the matter of an amanuensis, the regulations are silent.

One is entitled to infer from the silence that it is permissible to charge for this service. Having said that, I incline to the view that to do so would be contrary to the spirit of the law, even if it does not infringe the letter. I hardly think that it would show the school in a very good light.

4

Staff absence and cover

Absence from work is a more serious problem in teaching than in most other types of employment. A teacher's work cannot simply be left to pile up on the desk until he or she returns, though of course some of it does. The pupils are there and they need someone to supervise them and preferably to continue with their education. Questions relating to absence of staff and how it can be covered rank high among the daily concerns of Heads and especially Deputies, upon whom the burden of resolving the problems most often falls.

Absence because of illness or accident is one thing and that has largely been covered in Chapter 3. There are other kinds of absence to contend with as well.

Q. What are the rules for granting leave of absence, with or without pay, for teachers?

A. Leave of absence falls into two categories, namely contractual rights provided for in the Burgundy Book, the record of agreements made by all LEA employers with the teachers' unions, which cover such issues as maternity leave and absence for public duties, and minor cases, such as compassionate leave for the illness or death of close relatives.

The terms set out in the Burgundy Book are part of the contractual conditions of service of all teachers in LEA-maintained schools and many grant-maintained and independent schools have adopted similar terms. The minor cases have normally been left to the discretion of the individual employer, although they have often been the subject of agreements between employers and teachers at the LEA level or of regulations made by LEAs. Typically, these will indicate which categories of absence may be granted with pay and which without and for how long. Some allow discretion under certain conditions to Heads. Under Local Management of Schools, this may be delegated to school level and, where this is the case, governing bodies should draw up their own policies. Independent and grant-maintained schools should also have their own policies. Where Heads are able to exercise discretion in granting leave of absence, they should try to be consistent in their rulings.

Q. Are teachers exempt from jury service?

A. No. Given the need for educated and experienced citizens to serve on juries, it would be unfortunate to exempt such a large category of people from this vital public service.

At the same time, there are circumstances, for instance with classes preparing for public examinations, where the absence of a teacher for a prolonged period might have serious consequences for students. The courts are generally very understanding about such situations and a teacher who is summoned to serve at a difficult time should write to the court explaining the circumstances and asking for them to be considered.

Q. What are the rules relating to leave of absence to attend funerals of relatives?

A. This is a matter to be determined by the employer at his discretion. Many LEAs have policies on this, which have been negotiated by the unions over the years. Some of these are detailed and precise, even going into categories of consanguinity, while others leave a measure of discretion to Heads. Grant-maintained schools and LMS schools, which have not adopted the LEA policy as their own, would do well to establish at least an outline policy on this matter.

While it is desirable that the Head should have discretion in dealing compassionately with individual cases, it is helpful to have general guidelines within which to work, in order to avoid embarrassing situations and the setting of precedents which may be subsequently regretted.

In all state schools, the number of days on which the school must be open to pupils is fixed at 190, with five additional days when the staff must be available for work without the pupils, usually for the purposes of their own professional training and development. Denominational schools are not exceptions to these regulations:

Q. Given that Local Education Authorities determine the 195 days in the year when teachers must be available for work, what provision is made for paid religious holidays?

A. A decision taken by a denominational school to observe a religious holiday does not remove the obligation to work 195 days. The additional day will have to be made up during the course of the year.

This explanation immediately sparked off a further question:

Q. In the light of your reply on religious holidays, do teachers who are granted leave for such days have to make up their time out of term?

A. I am afraid you have confused two issues here. My previous comments were meant to apply to schools which close for a religious festival and not to individuals granted leave of absence. It is in the former case that the school must observe the requirement to be open to pupils for 190 days during the year.

In the latter case, when individuals are granted leave of absence, the situation is exactly similar to leave on compassionate grounds or for moving house. The school remains open and so no demand is made for additional attendance by those who have been absent. Whether the absence is granted with pay or without it depends upon circumstances. Most are with pay, under the terms of standing agreements between employer and employee, which are part of Conditions of Service.

If it is the Head who is away, there is an additional consideration: someone has to take charge of the school:

Q. If there are two Deputies in the school, which of them takes charge when the Head is away?

A. It is part of the duty of a Head to ensure that a Deputy, or other suitable person, is designated to take charge when he or she is away. This may be done as a permanent arrangement, or on a rota, or ad hoc on each occasion.

In my view, a Head should lay down clearly what the policy is, so that there can be no ambiguity in an emergency. Many Deputy Heads have the duty included in their job description, or are clearly designated as First Deputy, so avoiding any possible confusion.

Absence for a day or two is one thing, but prolonged absence may mean not only that someone has to be found to teach the classes left without their teacher, but also, if that absentee carries additional responsibilities, that another member of the staff has to pick up those duties. Inevitably, that raises the question of being paid for it.

Q. My Head of Department was absent ill all last term and it looks likely that he will not return for some time yet. I have been looking after the job in his absence. When should I become entitled to be paid for doing so?

A. Most LEAs lay down rules for this which specify the period of absence after which an acting allowance becomes payable. The period varies from one LEA to another, but, if yours is an LEA-maintained school, you should enquire what the local position is. If you are in a grant-maintained school, your governing body should have a policy. If they have not, you should persuade the teacher-governors to raise the matter.

A teacher taking on a post for more than a term should certainly be entitled to receive appropriate remuneration and I recommend that you discuss the matter with your Head at an early date.

Because, in accordance with the *School Teachers' Pay and Conditions of Service Document*, there are limitations upon the amount of cover for absent colleagues which teachers can be called upon to undertake, most cover duty is undertaken by temporary teachers, commonly called 'supply teachers', who are employed on a casual basis for the purpose.

Good supply teachers are rare and a school which finds them will do its best to keep quiet about it, so that they are not used elsewhere. Many are regarded as unsatisfactory. They are unfamiliar with the pupils and with the work they are doing. There is little time to brief them when they arrive and pupils need few excuses to exploit the situation. Some schools have tried to find alternative solutions:

Q. Is it possible to use permanent staff for cover duties in school instead of bringing in supply teachers?

A. Certainly. I am assuming that the plan is to allow certain staff to have a lighter timetable than the generality and to assign them to cover for absent colleagues as required, so making up the difference.

There is much to be said for the idea, not least that the teachers providing the cover will be familiar to the pupils and aware of what is required. You may have problems, unless their regular timetable is very light indeed, of meeting all your cover needs in this way.

Finding supply teachers is often a time-consuming and frustrating business. I well remember an LEA list on which all those named seemed to be either dead, heavily pregnant or moved out of the area. Some schools have, therefore, turned to one of the many agencies which have sprung up in recent years who offer to do the job for you. It is no cheaper for the school, but the agency makes its profit by paying lower rates (see p.69).

Since the introduction of delegated budgets, schools have become acutely conscious of the cost of supply teachers and have made strenuous efforts to keep the bill as low as possible. This may sometimes put pressure on the staff:

Q. During the examination period and after, many teachers are relieved of teaching duties. Can they be used to cover for absent colleagues, even after three days of absence ?

A. Possibly. The School Teachers' Pay and Conditions of Service Document allows this to happen where a teacher is required to teach for less than 75 per cent of the normal teaching day. Some teachers, with large commitments to examination classes may well fall into this category. On the other hand, they may also be required to invigilate the examinations.

Q. *Our Head has expressed concern about staff absences, including hospital appointments and examination moderation meetings. He is particularly unhappy about female staff absent because their own children are sick. Can a Head refuse to provide cover for staff absences of this kind?*

A. Refusing cover is not really the point here, because a Head's first duty is to ensure the welfare and safety of pupils and that means that an absent teacher has to be covered by someone, unless the pupils are to be sent home.

Many Heads are seriously concerned about the amount of absence caused by the requirements of moderation of school-based examinations and coursework, in spite very often of their belief that this style of examination is beneficial to pupils. Examination boards need to pay more attention to their requirements in this respect and, in particular, they need to allow schools the flexibility which would minimize the need to interrupt teaching and learning.

The other issue you raise is quite different. It may not be a popular thing to say but, when teachers, male or female, accept positions, their first commitment, during their directed time of work, is to the pupils they are paid to teach and not to their own children. Those who have young children should, therefore, ensure that arrangements are in place for them to be looked after in the event of their being unwell. While absence to deal with an emergency can always be accepted on compassionate grounds, continuing absence to mind sick children cannot.

Your Head is quite right to express concern, but he should be doing something about it, first by reminding the teachers concerned of the terms of their contract and second by warning them that they cannot expect to be paid for unauthorized absence.

The pressure is on Heads, too, who may find their concern for the budget in conflict with their desire to be kind and understanding:

Q. When a teacher is absent from school on compassionate grounds, in this case for bereavement, are his colleagues required to cover for him for as long as it takes?

A. Most schools will have a policy for granting compassionate leave, but often leave it to the Head's discretion to allow a longer period than the rules stipulate in particular cases.

The arrangements for cover are no different from those which normally operate, namely that teachers are not required to cover after the teacher who is absent or unavailable has been so for three or more consecutive days. If the fact of the absence, which was going to last for three or more days, was known to the school at least two working days before it commenced, they would not be required to cover at all.

Even leave of absence without pay may have a hidden cost:

Q. Under LMS, should the LEA pay for the cost of cover when a teacher is granted leave of absence without pay?

A. Leave of absence without pay is calculated on the same basis as absence because of illness; that is, that one day is worth one three hundred and sixty-fifth of salary. Cover is calculated on a daily rate of one one hundred and ninety-fifth of salary. Thus, you are unlikely to receive back sufficient to provide the cover cost for the absence, unless your LEA, in a moment of unwonted generosity, decreed otherwise in their LMS scheme.

Of course, if you managed to arrange cover for the absent teacher without taking on staff, your school budget is in profit. You may well wish to scrutinize any application for unpaid leave more carefully than heretofore.

The cost of absence also includes sick-pay. Some LEAs have retained the costs of long-term absence as a central item, so that schools do not bear the full brunt. This is by no means universal practice, however, and school budgets have to contain an element of contingency to cover such eventualities. It is important to know how sick-pay is calculated, even if the LEA actually handles the payroll.

Q. We have had a teacher on sick-leave since last February, apart from a brief spell back in June. Do we calculate his sick-pay from the first day of his absence?

A. I assume that your school is either an LEA school or one which is operating under the conditions of service agreements, known collectively as the Burgundy Book.

The agreement on sick-pay entitles the sick teacher to receive sick-pay at full pay or half pay for prescribed periods, depending on the length of service, within any one year. For anyone with four years or more of service, this provides full pay for 100 working days and half pay for a further 100 working days.

The year, for the purposes of these calculations, commences on 1 April. The additional provision, which is interesting in your case, is that, where a teacher is absent sick on 31 March, his continued absence after that date is deemed to be part of the preceding year. Thus, your absentee, assuming he has at least four years of service, was entitled to full pay from his first day of absence until his return in June and then, when he went sick again, the calculation began again at that point, giving him an entitlement of six months on full pay thereafter.

Teachers should be aware of the rules relating to sick-pay and also to other conditions of service matters, such as maternity leave and benefits. I end this chapter with a cautionary tale, which has affected more than one unsuspecting teacher.

Q. I took up my present position in an LEA school earlier this year, having previously served in a grant-maintained school. I am now pregnant and I have just been informed that I have minimal entitlement to maternity benefit, in spite of my nine years of service. What has happened to women's rights?

A. Nothing – but I am afraid you have not taken sufficient note of the small print in relation to your most recent appointment.

Maternity rights, in common with other employment rights, are acquired as a result of continuous service with one employer and they are not transferred from one employer to another. In the case of teachers employed by local authorities, there is an agreement that service with one LEA will be treated as continuous on transfer to another. So, if you had moved from one LEA-controlled school to another, you would have preserved your rights.

You would even have preserved your rights, had you moved from LEA to grant-maintained, because GM schools adopted that arrangement to retain the goodwill of their teachers.

Unfortunately, this does not automatically apply to the reverse move, which you have made. Many LEAs have chosen to accept continuity but some, possibly motivated by their opposition to the whole concept of GM schools, have not. This point would have been set out in your contract when you were appointed to your present post.

5
Pay and conditions

The pay and conditions of schoolteachers are based on national arrangements, part statutory and part negotiated, locally administered. A brief historical explanation will provide the framework.

Until 1987, the salaries of all schoolteachers in the state system were negotiated between the representatives of the various unions and of the local education authorities who employed them, sitting in a body known as the Burnham Committee. Their agreements – or, as often happened, arbitrated awards when they failed to agree – were approved by the Secretary of State for Education and given statutory force by regulations laid before Parliament. Because most of the pay-bill was funded by government grant to local authorities, in practice the government played a key part behind the scenes of the negotiations, one of the many aspects of the system which were unsatisfactory and frustrating.

Conditions of service were tackled quite separately in negotiations with the employers, resulting in voluntary agreements, which were recorded in a document known universally as the Burgundy Book, a reference to its colour rather than to wine or place.

The frustrations of the Burnham Committee eventually proved too much for the government and it was abolished in 1987, to be replaced, after an interim period, by a Pay Review Body, whose annual reports are, if the Secretary of State accepts them, embodied in statutory regulations as before. Since 1987, however. some aspects of conditions of service, including the definitions of working time and duties, have come within the purview of the Review Body and become part of the statutory framework. Each year's settlement is embodied in the *School Teachers' Pay and Conditions of Service Document.*

Those aspects of conditions of service which had been recorded in the Burgundy Book have, however, remained much as they were. These include, for example, provisions relating to sick-pay, maternity leave and facilities for union representatives.

The Document applies to all teachers employed in state schools, except City Technology Colleges and any schools which have decided to take up an option of devising their own arrangements outside the system. The Burgundy Book applied to all employees in LEA schools, who were party to the agreements – Bromley and Derbyshire abstained – and many grant-maintained schools have accepted its terms, either because they inherited them or because it was easier to do so than to try to negotiate their own specific agreements.

In theory, the existence of the two documents should solve all problems about pay and conditions: the 'Helpline' postbag indicated that it did not entirely succeed. Although every school should possess copies, some enquiries revealed that teachers either had not read them or did not understand them. Others were seeking interpretations of the small print.

One reform which has made the process of salary calculation more accessible to teachers was the introduction of an annual review of all salaries:

Q. Are governors required to undertake an annual review of the salaries of all teachers or is it something they may do if they wish or can afford to do?

A. Since September 1993, bodies responsible for determining salaries of teachers, usually the governors, have a duty to conduct a review every year and to provide each teacher with a statement of what the salary is and how it has been calculated. They are required to do this within the context of a previously agreed salaries policy which applies to all staff.

The Department for Education and Employment, in its annual circular accompanying the *School Teachers' Pay and Conditions of Service Document*, provides guidance on the factors which ought to be taken into account in the course of the review.

The basis for calculating the salaries of all teachers is the standard pay spine for all teachers other than Heads and Deputies:

Q. I have heard that annual pay increments for teachers are no longer automatic. Is this true?

A. Not really. Annual increments for teachers below the maximum on the Standard Scale have never been completely automatic, in that there has always been a provision that the increment could be withheld, if service during the preceding year had been unsatisfactory. There are very few instances recorded when this has actually happened.

The School Teachers' Pay Review Body considered this issue last year, under pressure from the Department for Education, who wanted to make the increments dependent upon a performance review. In paragraph 81 of its 1993 Report, the Pay Review Body concluded:

> *'We see some force in the Department's arguments but they did not lead us to the same conclusion. Rather, we recommend that each year relevant bodies should be required to decide, on the advice of headteachers, whether any teacher in their employ has performed unsatisfactorily.'*

In practice, it seems unlikely that this will change things very much, although the fact that attention has been deliberately drawn to the possibility of withholding increments may lead to one or two cases.

These increments are, of course, those allowed for service. There are others awarded for additional responsibilities, up to two for work with pupils with special educational needs and, though these have been rarely used, for outstanding classroom performance. Once awarded or gained by service, these increments form part of the teacher's entitlement and may not be removed, while they remain in the same post. Service increments cannot be removed at all:

Q. When a teacher on the Standard Scale, who has received an additional increment, moves to a new post, is the new employer obliged to pay him at the same point?

A. Yes. The matter is dealt with in Appendix II, Section 1(3), of the *School Teachers' Pay and Conditions of Service Document,* where it is made clear that any teacher moving to a new post must be paid at a point on the Standard Scale no lower than the one he was on in his previous post.

Of course somebody quickly pointed out what appeared to be exceptions to the rule:

Q. You stated that a teacher moving from one LEA to another would not move down the Standard Scale. On moving from Bexley to Wiltshire, my daughter was placed on a lower point while doing daily supply work and is now on a lower rate in an FE job in the same county. Has she been wrongly treated?

A. I doubt it. Some LEAs now operate a separate arrangement for teachers employed on daily supply, setting a standard rate which does not relate to length of service. Had she taken a contractual post, the rules relating to placement on the scale would have applied. FE teaching is not governed by the *School Teachers' Pay and Conditions of Service Document*, but by the regulations negotiated for teachers in that sector. The salary level is not necessarily protected when a teacher transfers from one to the other.

It is not even permitted to give up an entitlement voluntarily, which is not quite so irrational as it might seem, because, were it allowed, some teachers might be browbeaten against their interests:

Q. I am a 36-year-old primary teacher who has been out of a job for nearly three years. All my many applications for jobs have proved unavailing. Should I offer to take a salary at a lower level in order to be employable?

A. I am very sorry indeed to learn of your plight, although I am, of course, unable to judge whether your failure to find a post is a matter of salary level or something else.

I would suggest that you should confide in a headteacher or local authority adviser whom you trust and ask him or her to review your application, in order to be sure that you are projecting yourself effectively. You would have to consider also whether those whose names you are giving as confidential referees are actually providing the kind of support you need to obtain interviews.

It may be that your fears are justified and that it is the salary level which is the difficulty. At present, there is little one can do about that: the rates of pay are laid down in the *School Teachers' Pay and Conditions of Service Document*, which has statutory force in all state schools. The only alternative might be in the private sector, where employers are not necessarily bound to adhere to those scales.

The protection of salaries when schools are reorganized is a common source of difficulty:

Q. Our school has diminished considerably in size, with the consequence that some teachers are holding incentive allowances at a higher level than the present school size justifies. Can we freeze the salary levels where they are now until the value of the lower incentive allowance catches up?

A. No. Where a school group size changes, whether because of a falling roll or of reorganization, the salaries of teachers who remain in post are protected at their current value, that is to say that a holder of an Incentive Allowance D, for example, is entitled to be paid a 'D' allowance for as long as he or she remains in that post in that school, whatever the cash value of that allowance may be. The post cannot be downgraded to a lower allowance for that incumbent, although it can for a replacement.*

The same principle applies to the salaries of Heads and Deputies, although not if they are placed on a spinal point outside the range appropriate to the group size of the school at the time when the salary was awarded.

Q. We have several teachers on the staff of the school where I am a governor who are sitting on protected salaries which they have had since a reorganization several years ago. The LEA, which originally paid for this, has now ceased to do so and we are faced with paying them in the context of serious budget problems. Can we reduce these salaries to what they should be?

---

*Since this answer was published, incentive alowances have been replaced by responsibility points. The answer is otherwise unaffected.

A. This is an increasing problem in many places and arises because, with the introduction of delegated budgets, many LEAs undertook to cover the costs of safeguarded posts for only a fixed period, after which, as in your case, the responsibility for finding the money devolved upon the school. The teachers concerned no doubt held posts commensurate with their salary in the past and lost them through no fault of their own. Section 21 of the *School Teachers' Pay and Conditions of Service Document* safeguards their salary at a level equivalent to what it was when the reorganization took place, unless they unreasonably refuse an offer of an alternative post at the same level or higher. This protection is statutory and no employer in the maintained sector may remove it unilaterally.

The first thing a governing body should do in these circumstances is to make sure that the Head is expecting from these teachers a level of performance and an acceptance of duties which match the salary. The enjoyment of protection does not exempt anyone from the need to work for it. The second priority is to be alert for opportunities for absorbing these teachers into the planned staffing structure, so that the protection, while not technically removed, becomes irrelevant.

The only other alternative, when faced with serious budgetary problems, is to consider redundancy, always bearing in mind that there may be other teachers on the staff who might be covered by the criteria which are established for determining redundancy and who have also to be considered before a decision is taken.

Protection can, however, cut both ways:

Q. How can one get staff who hold protected allowances to undertake responsibilities in return for those allowances?

A. This may be done simply by allocating responsibilities to them which are commensurate with the allowances they hold. There is nothing in the *School Teachers' Pay and Conditions of Service Document* which says that protection of salary implies that no duties may be allocated to match. A teacher is contractually obliged to work under the reasonable direction of the Head. The Head may, therefore, allocate such duties to teachers as he or she considers appropriate to their qualifications and experience, having regard to the general balance of work amongst all staff. Any teacher who believes that the duties allocated are unreasonable may have recourse to the grievance procedure but I find it hard to imagine that any panel hearing a grievance which was based on the premise of pay without the appropriate level of work would be much impressed thereby.

If it is specified at the time of appointment, a responsibility point does not have to be permanent:

Q. Under the pay structure, is it possible to award teachers temporary allowances for one term?

A. The current structure did away with the old system of allowances altogether, replacing it with the pay spine. There is nothing in the regulations which prevents a teacher being moved to a higher point on the spine on a temporary basis, something which might very properly happen when, for instance, there is a need to make an acting appointment pending the filling of a vacancy. In all cases, it is vital that the notification of the change makes it clear that it is for a limited period and for the reason specified.

Some schools have been concerned that the size of the steps between points of the pay spine is too large to allow staff to be given small but welcome temporary increases for specific tasks. This may be overcome with a little ingenuity. If, for example, the amount of money which governors wish to offer is about one-third of the difference between one point and the next, the temporary appointment can run for one term only, with the understanding that this is being given for work which will last the whole year.*

Having a statutory structure means that one cannot operate outside it, unless, of course, the school has entirely opted out of the system:

Q. Is it permissible to pay teachers honoraria for specific tasks or bonuses for jobs well done?

---

*In 1996, halfpoints were introduced, helping to resolve this problem.

A. It is not possible to do this in quite the way that is implied in your question, because all remuneration of teachers must be based upon the terms of the School Teachers' Pay and Conditions of Service Document. This makes no explicit allowance for payments such as you envisage.

It is possible to achieve your objective, however – or something very like it – by awarding temporary increments for fixed periods. You might decide, for example, to promote a teacher to one point on the spine above his or her current level for one term, having calculated that the salary increase which would be gained over that period would be roughly equivalent to what you wanted to pay.

If your governing body decides to act in this way, great care must be taken to ensure that the documentation dealing with the appointment is quite precise about the temporary and non-renewable nature of the promotion, so that potential misunderstandings are avoided.

Although the Document sets out how responsibility points are awarded, it does not give very clear guidance on what they can be given for. This allows schools to make their own judgements, but there are pitfalls:

Q. Under the pay scheme, can incremental enhancements be given for work outside 1265 hours?

A. There is nothing in the regulations which says that this cannot be done, but I am bound to say that I believe that it would be very ill-advised.

The principle upon which I base my argument is that it can never be sensible to be paying someone for doing something which one cannot direct them to do. In other words, if, for example, one informs a teacher that she is to receive an enhancement in recognition of the work she does out of school time with the girls' netball team, and the following week she announces that she is giving up that activity, there is nothing one can do to insist that she should continue with what is, by definition, a voluntary activity.

If, on the other hand, an enhancement is awarded in recognition of the general quality of the teacher's work and contribution to the school, one acknowledges all that is being done without making the specific link to the voluntary activity.

It is important to ensure that, when increments are awarded, they are given for real responsibility and not out of misguided kindness:

Q. One of my teachers is a single parent who is struggling to make ends meet. Can I recommend to the governors that he be given an increment in recognition of his straitened circumstances?

A. Your compassion does you credit, but I cannot advise you to do this.

The criteria for the award of incremental points are clearly set out in the *School Teachers' Pay and Conditions of Service Document* and there is no provision for operating outside them. If, of course, there are additional responsibilities which would merit an increment and which he is competent to take on, you might achieve your aim that way.

The reality is, however, that you are managing a school, not a charity, and you have a duty to ensure that all the resources at the school's disposal are used to further the education of pupils. The argument that relief from financial worry might make this man a better teacher is too tenuous to be acceptable.

Part-time teachers can be a particular headache when applying the terms of the Document:

Q. As a part-time teacher, I have 11 hours of work spread over three days in the week. Can I be required to attend a regular staff meeting which occurs on one of the other days?

A. That depends entirely upon the terms of your contract, or letter of appointment, which lays down the terms on which you are employed. A part-time teacher has 'directed time' in accordance with the proportion of full time for which he or she is employed.

If, however, you are employed on an hourly basis and not as a proportion of full-time, you may be required to attend and to work only for those hours for which you are paid. If you are required to attend meetings, then you can expect to be paid for doing so.

Even if you are employed for a proportion of full time, the expectation that you should attend a meeting on a day when you are not otherwise required might be resisted on the grounds that it was unreasonable, a point which you could establish, if necessary, by the use of the grievance procedure.

Q. What are the rules governing the attendance of part-time teachers on INSET days?

A. There are no specific rules as such, because it must be assumed, unless otherwise specified in the contract, that a part-time teacher is committed to attend on training days in exactly the same way and in the same proportion as on the other 190 working days in the year.

In practice, there may well be scope for negotiation so that the prescribed proportion of full time is served on the training days so as to fit in with the training needs of the teacher and the way in which the training is organized. It has to be by negotiation, however, because the teacher may well have domestic arrangements or other commitments built around the part-time contract, which make an adjustment difficult to arrange.

Q. Can a part-time teacher be given an allowance above Standard Scale for extra responsibilities?

A. Certainly. There is nothing in the *School Teachers' Pay and Conditions of Service Document* to prevent it. If such an allowance were awarded, one would expect it to be paid pro rata in proportion to the part-time working.

The following question revealed another rather different aspect of part-time work:

Q. We have been instructed by the Department of Social Security that our part-time visiting instrumental teachers cannot be self-employed, as they would like to be. Are we obliged to put them on the payroll?

A. Yes, you are. This is more a matter for the Inspector of Taxes, who has strict rules about what can and cannot constitute self-employment. The essential point here is that, even though the pupils may be paying for their tuition, the teachers are not entering into a private contract with them or with their parents but with the school. So, while the teachers may be self-employed in respect of private tuition provided on their own premises, when they come into school to work, they must be treated as employees.

The employment of teachers on supply can also be a cause of misunderstanding, because of the differing terms on which they are employed:

Q. Could you explain the difference between what local authorities pay for supply teachers and what agencies pay to those they take on? Are those agencies which pay a flat rate breaking the law?

A. Supply teachers employed under the *School Teachers' Pay and Conditions of Service Document* should be paid at a rate related to the point to which they are entitled, by virtue of qualification and experience, on the pay spine. This makes some supply teachers more expensive than others and there is a view that a fixed rate might be more appropriate. At present, however, all schools which have not adopted their own pay structure and all local authorities are bound by the rules.

Agencies who place supply teachers are not themselves bound by these rules and they need not, therefore, pass on to the staff they employ the full rate paid to them. If supply teachers work through an agency, they accept whatever terms the agency offers: if they do not like them, they need not join them.

Q. I know of a case of a teacher who has taken maternity leave and returned to her post in the second week of July, thus drawing her full pay for the summer holidays and depriving the teacher who has covered for her of any holiday pay. Can nothing be done to rectify this injustice?

A. There is no injustice here. The maternity regulations have no regard to the accident of school holiday dates and a woman is entitled to return to her post at the prescribed time after the birth of her baby. The idea that she is drawing holiday pay is a misconception: teachers are paid an annual salary, which is divided into twelve monthly instalments without consideration of when holidays occur.

Equally, there is no injustice to the temporary teacher who covered for the maternity leave. He or she will have been engaged either on a fixed-term contract, specified to terminate at the conclusion of the maternity leave, or, if it has not been the same person continuously, on a daily supply rate. The latter rate is calculated on the basis of 195 days in the year, the number of days a teacher is required to work, and he or she will have received one one hundred and ninety-fifth of the relevant full salary for each day worked. In neither case does the concept of holiday pay apply.

The question of so-called holiday pay comes up in various guises:

Q. Can we save money by employing a temporary teacher only up to the last day of the summer term, rather than paying for six weeks' summer holiday?

A. That depends upon the nature of the engagement of the teacher and the length of time for which you are employing him or her.

If the teacher is being employed for a short period on a daily rate, then you are obliged only to pay for the days worked. If, however, the teacher is employed for the whole term, then you must pay for the whole term, which is calculated to include the holiday period. The agreement on Teachers' Conditions of Service, contained in the so-called Burgundy Book, specifies that a teacher must be paid no less than one-third of the appropriate annual salary for a full term's work.

In practice, it does not make as much difference as you may have imagined, because payment on a daily rate is calculated on the basis of 195 days, whereas payment on a termly basis is calculated on the basis of 365 days.

Q. You did not answer fully the question about temporary teachers working in the summer term. I was asked to teach on a contract up to the end of May and I then continued on a supply basis until July, thus losing any entitlement to holiday pay. Is this legal, acceptable or normal?

A. The practice you describe is legal. Whether it is acceptable is up to the teacher who accepts the position. As I endeavoured to point out in my earlier answer, the calculation of the daily rate for supply teaching is based on 195 days in the year, so that for one day you receive one one hundred and ninety-fifth of a full salary. On a short-term contract, paid by the month, you receive one twelfth of a full salary each month, whether you work on each weekday of that month or not. Both calculations take holidays into account.

From a school's point of view, it makes sense to employ a teacher on a daily supply basis in the summer term because a short-term contract, which would terminate on 31 August, might turn out to be more expensive than the daily supply costs. Given, too, that, in secondary schools, examinations end well before the end of the summer term, this policy represents shrewd management of the school's resources. There is no rule which gives a temporary teacher an entitlement to six weeks' holiday with pay and, frankly, I cannot see that there should be.

The salaries of Heads and Deputies are calculated on a different basis from those of other teachers and their statutory conditions are also different, most notably in that their hours of work are not defined. The salary structure also differs in that, while there is a pay spine, there is no incremental progression from point to point on it. Instead, it is up to the relevant body, usually the governors, to determine, subject to certain limits, the point on the spine appropriate to each individual.

The limits define the range of points within which the governors must operate, unless there are exceptional reasons for not doing so, and are based on School Groups.

Q. I am puzzled by the Group numbers of schools which I see advertised in the TES. The Group seems to bear little relation to the number on roll. Can you explain why this should be so?

A. The Group to which a school is allocated is the outcome of a calculation of what is called its Unit Total. Each pupil is worth a number of units, depending on age. Under 14-year-olds are worth 2 units, under 15s 4, under 16s 5, under 17s 7 and 17 and over 9. The sum of all the units in the school is the Unit Total, which is used to determine the ranges of salaries appropriate for the Head and Deputy Heads.

It will be apparent from this that a school which has a large sixth form will have a higher Unit Total than another school which has no sixth form but maybe a larger roll. Differences of this kind are reflected in the apparent discrepancies you have noticed.

The salary ranges for the six groups overlap, both for Heads and Deputies:

Q. I am a Deputy Head in a school which is about to move from Group 5 to Group 6. My salary is near the top of the range for Group 5. Does the upgrading entitle me to a salary increase?

A. Of itself, no. The only application of the School Group system now is for the determination of the salaries of Heads and Deputies, although the salary ranges for all groups overlap. Thus, your current salary is at the lower end of the range for Group 6. The governors are not, therefore, obliged to increase salary, unless they are persuaded that there is a case for doing so.

Your salary, like those of all staff, must be reviewed annually and you may wish to make a particular case this year on the grounds that the change of group reflects an increase in the number of pupils and thus an increase in the burden of managerial and administrative duties which you have to undertake. You may find that your governors are operating a policy of fixing the salaries of the Head and Deputies at a particular level within the relevant range. If so, you may benefit that way.

As with teachers' salaries, the rules may not be broken, although a little bending may be in order:

Q. In determining the salary of the Head, is it possible for the governors to set a figure between the spine points given in the School Teachers' Pay and Conditions of Service Document?

A. No. The Document has statutory force and heads and teachers generally can only be remunerated in accordance with the scales set out. Although the salaries of heads and deputies have been negotiable within the prescribed ranges since 1991, governors are not allowed to introduce their own variations.

The only way in which an increase which is effectively less than a full point can be made is by making a temporary increase of a whole point for a limited period, say for one term. Governors might feel that this could be justified in particular circumstances, such as a major reorganization or building programme.

The introduction of an element of negotiation at this level has not been popular with everyone and it has led to a considerable variation in the salaries of Heads and Deputies doing comparable jobs, the differences not always being readily attributable to considerations of merit.

Q. Is it now possible to negotiate one's salary when applying for a headship?

A. That is a matter for the appointing panel and the governing body concerned. If, in the advertisement for the post or in the distributed material, it is made clear that the salary level is not negotiable, at least one knows where one stands. If the matter is left unclear, there is no reason why a candidate should not raise it at interview. It would probably be best to do so either informally or at a preliminary interview, rather than at the last minute. If the salary level is to be a factor in determining whether you wish to accept the post, if offered, it is as well to know the position early on.

Once in post, the possibility of obtaining a rise exists with each annual review, although, unless governors handle matters with care, there is a considerable risk of controversy and dispute.

Q. The governors of this school have just moved the Head's salary three points up the spine and the Deputies only two, thus increasing the differential between them. Are they able to make arbitrary decisions like this?

A. Yes, I am afraid they are, although they ought not, in fact, to be entirely arbitrary.

Decisions on pay for all staff should be based on a salaries policy which should set out the criteria to guide the committee which deals with individual salaries. Most governing bodies stick pretty closely to the criteria given in the *School Teachers' Pay and Conditions of Service Document* and consider the guidance given in the accompanying Circular. From your point of view, it is useful to note that governing bodies are advised to consider carefully the question of differentials between the salaries of Heads and Deputies and between the latter and the next highest paid teachers.

Anyone dissatisfied with the decision of the committee may appeal to the governing body and be heard by an appeals committee, with a different membership. This would give one an opportunity to raise issues of fairness and differentials and to question the application of the criteria to the particular case. As very few people are their own best advocates in matters of this kind, you might wish to involve your professional association to support you.

The fact that the working time of Heads and Deputies is not defined can be a cause for concern in various ways. The lack of a prescribed limit may not be a help to those who are natural 'workaholics', but there are some who would seem to see it differently:

Q. Although Heads and Deputies are not covered by the limit of 1265 hours of directed time, what would you consider to be a reasonable percentage of that time for Heads and Deputies to be absent from their work-place on other 'professional duties'?

A. You might as well enquire about the length of a piece of string! First of all, when a Head or Deputy is performing professional duties off the school premises, they may be absent from their workplace, but they are certainly not absent from work. These days, the demands of school leadership have imposed more and more tasks upon Heads and Deputies, all of them quite legitimate in themselves, which cumulatively take them out of school much more than was once thought necessary or even wise.

There are many examples one could cite, but obvious ones include liaison with other schools, developing education–industry links, promoting the school in the local community and appraising professional colleagues elsewhere. Consultations with the local education authority, attending briefings on new education legislation, attending juvenile courts to support pupils in trouble and case conferences with the Social Services Department may also take up a great deal of time.

Every Head has a constant struggle to balance these important demands against the need to keep the school firmly under supervision and to meet the expectations of staff, pupils and parents, who want attention immediately and not when an appointment can be arranged. For most, the answer lies in a well-thought-out and well-understood system of delegation at the senior level and the operation of an effective senior management team, in which each member enjoys the confidence of the Head in acting on his or her behalf .

If I am right in detecting a note of criticism in your question, I hope you will give some thought to the very wide range of tasks which Heads and Deputies are expected to perform. I suspect that most of them work hours well in excess of 1265 anyway, and few of them find the time to count them.

The heavy burden of headship may have prompted one very unusual question:

Q. Is it legally possible to have job-sharing in the post of headteacher?

A. The concept of job-sharing has no foundation in law: it is an example of good employment practice which provides opportunities, most commonly for women with young children, for people to take jobs which would not otherwise be open to them. In reality, job-sharing is simply the division of one post into two part-time appointments in an arrangement where the two employees, who may or may not divide the work equally, work together to ensure that the full requirements of the position are delivered. It is for the employer to determine whether a particular post is capable of being filled in this way and there is no legal compulsion upon him to do so. Each case should be decided on its merits.

The concept has been applied with apparent success to teaching posts in schools, where it is for the Head, governors or LEA, as the case may be, to decide whether to accept it. I know of no instance where it has been applied to headship and I do not believe that it would be acceptable. The post of headteacher is the only one specifically required by regulation (Education (Teachers) Regulations, 1989) and this refers to it in the singular.

The legal responsibilities of headship are not, in my view, capable of being shared, even if the resultant confusion in the minds of teachers, parents and pupils could be overcome.

There are sometimes problems, both relating to pay and otherwise, when leaving one post and taking up another.

Q. A teacher who left this school at the end of the summer term started in a new post before 31 August. Will she be paid twice for those days?

A. Under the agreement between employers and teachers contained in the Burgundy Book, a teacher resigning to take up an appointment with another authority or another maintained school is paid up to the day preceding the day on which the new school opens for the start of the Autumn term, if this is earlier than 1 September.

If the teacher in question is working outside the maintained sector, then she may just be lucky!

Q. Can a resignation once submitted be withdrawn?

A. Lord Palmerston was said to have had a desk-drawer full of resignations from his Chancellor, Mr Gladstone, and it was his skill at man-management which kept them there. Many Heads will have their own Gladstones and will handle them in a similar way.

It is true, however, that a written resignation is an indication of intention to terminate a contract and, if it is accepted by the employer, a subsequent change of mind does not necessarily restore the contract. If the employer has accepted it in good faith and has made fresh dispositions accordingly, there is no obligation upon him to give way. He will, however, need to consider whether the original resignation was delivered under abnormal stress and would, if accepted, leave the employer open to challenge on grounds of constructive dismissal.

There are some who would like to take a short cut:

Q. I have been offered a very attractive post at another school, but they want me to start in September. Can I ask my present school to waive the period of notice?

A. You can ask, but they do not have to agree. The requirements for notice of resignation are a part of your contract and are there to protect you as well as your employer from last-minute decisions. As a contract represents a legally binding agreement between two parties, it follows that no part of it can be waived, except where both parties are willing to do so.

It is not uncommon for the requirement of notice to be waived, particularly when dealing with retirement on health grounds or where both parties find that doing so serves their interests. In a case like yours, however, when your present school fears that its teaching programme for the following term will be disrupted by your late departure, they are well within their rights to insist upon your contract being observed. The other school will fully understand this situation and, while it was worthwhile trying to persuade your present school to be generous, they should accept the situation and be prepared to wait a term until you are free to join them.

Finally, one cannot forget that there are other employees apart from teachers and their salary structures and conditions of service are likely to be entirely different from those applicable to teachers. Here are just two examples:

Q. The LEA has informed us that we are not allowed to pay our Senior Administrative Officer overtime, even though it is sometimes necessary for her to work extra hours to cope with the workload. I thought that governing bodies decided these things now. Must we still obey the LEA?

A. In this case, you must. Although you have not said so, I assume that the salary grade of this officer is on the APT & C local government scale, at a level which is not directly related to hours and therefore overtime cannot be defined. In other words, her situation is similar to that of the Head and Deputies, who receive fixed salaries, regardless of how many hours they put in.

If you have established a fixed working week for the SAO, the only way to resolve your problem is to allow her time off in lieu when the pressure of work is lighter.

Q. What are the rules governing the pay of classroom assistants?

A. Laboratory and workshop technicians are paid under Local Government A P & T Scales, which are the subject of agreements between employers and unions. The classroom assistants may be placed under the same heading by the LEA, if your school is an LEA school. Otherwise, you may find that you have a relatively free hand in the matter.

As this chapter has shown, the Head of a school needs to be a well-trained personnel manager, with a good understanding of salary structures and conditions of service as well as the skills needed to handle a well-educated and articulate workforce, some of whom may well be easily convinced that they are unfairly treated. It is all the more important to remember that the prime task is to ensure that children learn and fulfil their potential. The management of pay and conditions must serve that goal.

6

Pensions

Pensions might, at first glance, be seen as a subject of interest only to the individual, but familiarity with the pensions system is an essential requirement of good management. A good working knowledge is important for supporting and advising individual teachers and for managing complex staffing problems.

At one time, all teachers were obliged to belong to the Teachers' Superannuation Scheme, administered by the government and funded by contributions from teachers themselves and from their employers. In the interests of market freedom, teachers were allowed to opt out of the scheme in the 1980s and some were persuaded to do so by insurance companies, who sold plans some of which later proved to be highly disadvantageous to those who joined them. In some cases, compensation was paid to those who had been wrongly advised and they rejoined the teachers' scheme.

Although the management of this has now been privatized, the essential features of the scheme remain unchanged and are guaranteed by the government. Most teachers take the existence of the scheme for granted and few would be able to offer more than the haziest idea of what it provides for them, until, that is, they reach their fiftieth birthday or face some other personal crisis which focuses their attention on their personal financial future.

The first point to make about the scheme is that it is a contributory scheme, which means that all calculations are based on reckonable service, which is simply that period, or periods, of service for which contributions have been paid. Some people confuse this with actual working life or with periods of service which are admitted for calculation of salary, although they were not contributory to pension entitlement.

Q. *Why is my service in teaching abroad not taken into account in calculating my pension, when it was allowed in determining my salary in this country?*

A. Very simply, this is because the Teachers' Pension Scheme is a contributory scheme which entitles you to the benefits for which you and your employers have paid over the years. When you were teaching abroad, you were not contributing to the scheme and so you receive no benefit.

If you were allowed incremental credit on your salary for your service overseas, this was because your employer in this country decided that your experience justified that increase, but that decision has no bearing on your pension entitlement.

With the freedom to choose, teachers should be aware of the benefits which any pension scheme has to offer. As many of those who opted out belatedly discovered, the teachers' scheme has a number of features which were not replicated in private plans.

Q. *I hope to qualify and take up a teaching post in September. Should I join the Teachers' Pension Scheme, which I hear is to be privatized, or establish a private pension plan ?*

A. It is not for me to provide independent financial advice and you should certainly take advice from a qualified adviser and consult whichever of the teachers' unions you decide to join.

I can, however, offer some comments on the Teachers' Pension Scheme, which may be helpful. While it is true that the Teachers' Pension Agency, which administers the scheme, is to be privatized, it is the administration which is being privatized, rather than the funding of it, which remains guaranteed by the government. Pledges have been given by ministers that the essential features of the scheme itself will not be affected.

The single most important feature of the scheme is that the value of the eventual pension is linked annually with inflation. Of course, a successful private scheme might outperform inflation by bonuses, but this cannot be guaranteed and certainly not predicted long in advance.

The scheme has a number of other attractive features, including the opportunity to buy in added years for pension purposes.

By a lump sum payment, or by additional contributions made over time, one can add to the number of years upon which the final calculation is based.

Only you can decide what is best for you and your dependents, present or future, but you should use the Teachers' Pension Scheme as a yardstick against which to measure any alternatives.

Sadly, there are some people who are forced to look at their financial situation in the most tragic of circumstances:

Q. I am a teacher in my thirties and I have been told by my doctor that I have a possibly fatal illness. If he is right, what will my wife and children get, if I am still in post when I die?

A. I am sorry indeed to learn of your illness and I advise you to consult your union or professional association, who will offer very positive support to you.

Assuming you are a member of the Teachers' Pension Scheme, the scheme provides a lump sum death grant, plus widow's and children's pensions. The death grant is the greatest of:

- one year's average salary;
- the increased lump sum which you would have received had you retired on grounds of ill-health;
- your accumulated contributions plus interest of three per cent.

The widow's pension is normally half that which you would have received. The same amount is available for two or more children in full-time education and half that for one child.

As I can give here only a very general picture, you should get in touch about your own situation with the Teachers' Pensions Agency, Mowden Hall, Darlington, Co. Durham, DL3 9EE. I am sure that you will find them very supportive and helpful.

Enquiries about early retirement on grounds of ill-health are more common. The scheme provides for this by granting additional years to those earned by contributions, up to a maximum of six and two-thirds years for those with 20 or more years of service behind them. This enhances both the lump sum and the annual pension benefit.

Although a precise calculation will be done by the Agency, a good employer or manager should be able to provide a good estimate of the likely outcome to a teacher who needs to know what the situation might be. This is done by taking the period of reckonable service, plus any added years purchased or credited for retirement on health grounds, multiplying this by the best salary figure of the most recent three years and dividing by 80.

Q. How does one go about seeking retirement from teaching on grounds of ill-health? Does one have to be absent from work for a prolonged period?

A. An application for retirement on grounds of ill-health is made to the Teacher's Pension Agency by the employer and must be accompanied by medical evidence provided by one's doctor or consultant, who must be satisfied that the applicant is not fit to continue to work as a teacher.

The first step is to discuss the matter with your doctor in order to ascertain whether he or she believes that your state of health is such as to allow him or her to provide the required report. In the case of physical conditions, this may be quite straightforward. In cases of mental illness and stress, where physical consequences are not obvious it may be more difficult.

If the doctor indicates support for the application, one should then discuss the matter with one's employer. For a teacher, this would normally be the Head; for the Head it would be the Chairman of Governors or an LEA officer. A union or professional association may well be able to offer helpful advice at this stage.

The employer will then make formal application to the TPA, submitting the medical report. The TPA may, if it wishes, seek a second medical opinion from a practitioner of its choice.

A decision will usually be made within four to six weeks and, if it is unfavourable, there is a right to appeal.

And then what happens?

Q. I have applied to the TPA for early retirement on the grounds of ill-health. If the TPA agrees, when do I actually leave and do I have a choice ?

A. The regulations on this specify that the date of retirement should be agreed between the employer and the employee and should be fixed within six months of the formal notification from the TPA. If that date is passed, the process has to be recommenced, with fresh medical evidence.

Normally, agreement is easily reached, choosing the next normal leaving date at the end of a school term, giving the contractual period of notice, as prescribed by the Burgundy Book. Those whose state of health permits, may seek to fix the date as close as possible to the end of the six-month period, in order to enjoy the maximum time on full pay. The employer could, however, give contractual notice for an earlier leaving date, if there was one.

Applying for early retirement is one thing; getting it is another, and schools should be careful not to jump the gun, even though the needs of the pupils are pressing:

Q. We have a teacher who has been absent, ill, for a long time and he has now applied to the Teachers' Pension Agency for early retirement on grounds of ill-health. May we advertise for a replacement in advance of the formal notification?

A. You may advertise if you wish, but you will not have a vacancy to fill, and you would be most unwise to make an appointment, unless and until he has resigned. He will not wish to do that until he knows that the application has been granted and you should bear in mind that the approval allows the actual date of leaving service to be agreed between employer and employee during a period of six months following notification.

Should the TPA decline to grant the application, you might be left in an embarrassing situation in which the teacher might claim that you were seeking to dismiss him unfairly. I think that you might also consider the effect on this man and his family of advertising the post at a time when they may be under considerable stress.

It is not altogether surprising that some of those who retire from teaching in poor health should recover quite quickly, once they are released from the daily stresses of the classroom. When that happens, their thoughts turn, whether for financial reasons or just because they miss it, to going back again, at least in a small way:

Q. At the end of last term, I took retirement on the grounds of ill-health. I am already feeling much better and would like to try a little part-time teaching. Will this affect my pension?

A. It might very well do so. If you went back to work in a pensionable post, your pension would be either suspended or reduced, depending on how much you were earning. When you eventually retired again, the additional service would be taken into account in recalculating your final pension.

In the case of part-time work, such as you are contemplating, much depends on the amount of time you propose to work. If you do six months or more at half-time, your pension will cease after six months. If you work for less than half-time, your pension will not be suspended, but it may be reduced.

Remember, too, that, as you have been medically certified as unfit to work as a teacher, your employer has to be satisfied that you are fit to come back.

Whatever you decide, you should obtain the guidance of the Teachers' Pension Agency, whose Leaflet 192 provides full information on this aspect of the system.

Q. I retired from teaching on the grounds of ill-health in 1989. I have undertaken some casual supply teaching since then. I was disturbed to read that the Secretary of State might require people in my position to have a further medical examination, which might lead to the cancellation of my pension. Is there any truth in this?

A. The DfEE guidelines on the Teachers' Superannuation Scheme say this:

> *'If your health has improved and your employer is satisfied that you are medically fit to resume teaching, the effect on your pension depends upon the type of employment undertaken.'*

In the past, the initiative in this has depended upon the teacher who expressed a desire to resume work and the rule is quite reasonable in this context.

There have been suggestions made recently that the Secretary of State wishes to take a somewhat tougher line on the administration of the superannuation scheme, because of the greatly increased number of teachers retiring early. Whether she would wish to go to the extent of forcing further medicals on those who had no desire to return to teach, I rather doubt, but, in cases where people are trying to have the best of both worlds by undertaking supply teaching while continuing to draw their pensions, I have some sympathy with the view that this could be seen as misusing the pension fund to which all teachers and their employers contribute.

Your retirement and the early release and enhancement of your pension were granted on the basis that you were unfit to work as a teacher. By undertaking supply work, you do raise a question about the validity of that assessment, even if you are only working part-time, and the Secretary of State has every right, if she so chooses, to check up on the state of your health.

There are some members of the profession who would like to depart early, but are not medically unfit:

Q. Can one leave teaching before the age of 60 without being declared unfit and still draw one's pension?

A. If you are a contributor to the Teachers' Pension Scheme, this can be achieved by being granted premature retirement 'in the interests of the efficient discharge of the employer's functions'.

This is possible if you are 50 or over and you are able to persuade your employers to allow you to retire and to certify that it is in the interests of the efficient discharge of their functions to do so. Given that it is unlikely to be in their interests to retain the services of someone who would rather not be there, it is unlikely that your employers would refuse to grant such a request, which would cost them nothing beyond the trouble of replacing you.

Even so, some people have problems:

Q. At 57, I feel that I can no longer cope adequately with my job as a Head and I should like to retire early. I cannot plead ill-health as a reason for going, but I could not contemplate doing so unless

I can draw my pension immediately. Although I am not seeking enhancement, my Chair of Governors says that she cannot grant my request. Has she the right to do this ?

A. Whether she has the right or not, she is clearly misguided. The Teachers' Pension Scheme, to which I assume you belong, allows for early retirement 'in the interests of the efficient discharge of the employer's functions'. Where the employer is prepared to certify this on an application for retirement, the Teachers' Pension Agency will, in all normal circumstances, allow the pension entitlement to be drawn immediately.

Although an employer might esteem one's services so highly as to seek to persuade one to stay, it is difficult to see how it could be in anyone's interests to retain someone who would much prefer not to be there. To accede to the application costs the employer nothing beyond the trouble of appointing a replacement and may even save money, if the resultant salary is lower. There is no interest served by your Chair's refusal: in the interests of common sense as well as common humanity, she should be invited to think again.

There is one more advantage of the Teachers' Pension Scheme which deserves a mention: the facility to continue to build up a pension, after leaving service, whether remaining in the country or going abroad.

Q. If I leave teaching for a couple of years and then return, can I continue to contribute to the Teachers' Pension Scheme?

A. Yes. The Teachers' Pension Agency allows those who leave the service temporarily to continue in the scheme, although you will have to pay both the employer's and employee's contributions, unless you are working for an employer who is willing to support you. Even so, you are responsible for the payment and the employer must pay through you.

If you are going to work as a teacher or supervisor abroad, you may be able to continue such an arrangement for up to six years. If you are staying in Britain, but not working as a teacher, the scheme may operate for three years. In neither case is it a necessary condition that you undertake to return to teaching in Britain.

You have to make a decision to stay with the scheme within six months of leaving in the first case and within three months in the second.

A point to bear in mind is that you can only contribute at the salary level you were at, plus any subsequent increases to that scale, when you left teaching.

You can find full details in Leaflet 721, available from the Teachers' Pension Agency, Mowden Hall, Darlington, DL3 9EE.

7

Redundancy

Ten years ago, no book on school management would have included a chapter on redundancy. Whatever other drawbacks a teaching career might have had, at least it was secure. Most teachers were employed by local authorities and, if schools were closed or were overstaffed, the authority simply redeployed the teachers to other schools in their area where there were vacancies. At a pinch, they would take them onto a central supply list to be sent out to cover for absences. Early retirement on favourable terms might well have been available to older teachers whose services were no longer required, but redundancy – that was for the cutthroat world of industry.

The introduction of delegated budgets and the transfer of most of the duties of employing staff to governing bodies changed all that virtually overnight. No school could afford to carry more staff than it needed, because it was obliged to balance its budget. No governing body was obliged to take on surplus staff from elsewhere when there was a vacancy: at best, they had a duty to consider such teachers, but, if they did not like them, they could reject them.

Some LEAs struggled to preserve the best features of the old system, a few with some success, thanks to voluntary agreements:

Q. Although our school is facing a considerable reduction in staffing, we are assured that our jobs will be safe, because there is a voluntary agreement on redeployment within the LEA. May we have confidence in this?

A. I should like to think so, but I must advise you to examine the nature of this agreement very carefully to see what guarantees it actually gives you.

Under LMS, the power to appoint staff is vested in the governing body of the school and they are free to do whatever they wish. In the case of Heads and Deputies, they are obliged by law to advertise posts nationally and could not, therefore, take a redeployed teacher at that level.

Voluntary agreements such as you describe exist in a number of LEAs and, in some, they appear to have worked quite well. The usual pattern is that the governing bodies of the participating schools agree to give prior consideration to teachers available for redeployment, before going into the open market. They are, however, not bound to appoint any of them and their decision is not open to challenge.

The crunch comes at the end of the school year when the potentially redeployed teachers have not found posts. Their current school cannot afford to have them back, but has not made them redundant, and the LEA has no funds available to take them onto central funding. That is why you need to read the small print in the agreement and that is why there are only a few such schemes working successfully.

Even where teachers are redeployed, this is often accompanied by a protection of salary, but this may prove to be no guarantee of security in the long run:

Q. When my former school went grant-maintained, the LEA encouraged teachers to apply for posts elsewhere, gave them 'redeployment status' and agreed to protect 'for ever' allowances that did not match posts after redeployment. Can the LEA back down from this promise, because of financial difficulties? Are the schools who received the redeployed teachers obliged to pay the protected salaries if the LEA does not, and are these teachers likely to be made redundant?

A. I very much fear that 'for ever' may be a more finite time than one would like to hope.

Without seeing the written statements in which the protection was promised, it is impossible to say just how binding it is upon the LEA. It may well not be a contractual obligation to the individual teachers concerned, but a commitment which was made to the schools where they are now employed, in terms of the local management of schools, to provide the funds to pay for the protected salaries, which enjoy that protection 'for ever' in the *School Teachers' Pay and Conditions of Service Document.* Even that 'for ever' could be changed if the Pay Review Body so recommended.

It is certainly possible that the LEA might find itself so short of funds that it was unable to go on providing the additional funding which was promised and you are right to suggest that, in those circumstances, the schools would be obliged to find the money out of their own budgets.

The next step could very well confirm your fears. If the school, in its turn, becomes strapped for cash, the governors are inevitably going to look at those teachers who hold allowances which are not part of their agreed structure and are therefore a drain on their resources. They would have to be careful in drawing up their criteria for redundancy, but it would be foolish to pretend that these protected teachers were not at greater risk than others in such an eventuality.

No employer likes to make people redundant. It is bad for morale, fraught with difficult managerial problems and damages the public image of the organization. Not surprisingly, therefore, governing bodies have looked for expedients which will help them to avoid the problem.

Q. Can we avoid getting into redundancy situations by issuing fixed-term renewable contracts?

A. This can work only in a very limited and short-term way. If you suspect that there is likely to be a need to reduce staff next year, but you have a vacancy to fill this year in an area where redundancy may well occur next, then it would be sound management sense to appoint someone on a fixed contract for one year.

If circumstances changed and you decided to renew that contract for a second year, the same situation would obtain up to the end of the second year, at which time the employee, having been employed in the same place for two years, would acquire the same employment rights as he or she would have if the post had been a permanent one. In other words, a temporary contract is an acceptable device for dealing with a temporary situation but not acceptable as a long-term means of getting around employment protection legislation.

The implications of this needed further explanation:

Q. We have employed a temporary teacher for two years, but we are now advertising to fill the post permanently. Are there any problems if the temporary teacher does not get the job?

A. Indeed there are. By serving for two years continuously, your temporary teacher will secure full rights under employment legislation. If the job goes to someone else, your governors are highly likely to face an action before an Industrial Tribunal for wrongful dismissal and with no defence to offer. They certainly cannot make the temporary teacher redundant, because there is a continuing demand for the work. An urgent rethink is needed here.

Once the idea of redundancy was established, some governing bodies thought that it might be used as a device for getting rid of people whom they did not want:

Q. A teacher who was appointed on a five-year contract to run a TVEI project is coming to the end of his term. His performance is less than brilliant and we should like to get rid of him and advertise in the hope of appointing someone better. The teacher's union is threatening to take us to an Industrial Tribunal. Should we do it anyway?

A. That depends on whether you want to be taken to the Industrial Tribunal, with every prospect of losing, or not. In spite of the fixed term, this teacher, by virtue of continuous service over two years, enjoys employment protection and could only be dismissed on the grounds of redundancy or unsatisfactory performance.

He clearly cannot be declared redundant, because you intend to fill the post anyway, and, to justify dismissal for poor performance, you would need to be able to demonstrate that appropriate warnings had been given, with opportunities for improvement, coupled with relevant support.

It is important to remember that, in dealing with redundancy, we are dealing with employment law which applies to all employers, not something exclusive to the world of state education. The advice which I had to give, therefore, applied just as much to independent schools as it did to the rest. They, too, were looking for devices to avoid redundancy:

Q. At our independent school, we are having to reduce our staffing because of the recession. What is the position when reducing a full-time teacher to part-time? Do we have to give a contractual period of notice?

A. The position is that, if the full-time teacher has been with you longer than two years, you cannot do this other than by voluntary negotiation or by redundancy.

Your governors might well consider the possibility of achieving the objective by offering the teacher compensation for the loss of the full-time contract of such an amount that it will be accepted voluntarily. This sum would obviously need to be more attractive than the statutory redundancy payment, to which the teacher would be entitled if you sought to terminate the contract unilaterally. In the case of a voluntary settlement, the period of notice can be part of the agreement but, in the case of redundancy, the teacher is entitled to such notice as is specified in the contract.

You should remember, too, that, if you are opting for a redundancy, you need to be sure that your criteria have been properly drawn up and publicized and that all those teachers who might be considered for redundancy have been taken into account. Failure to follow proper procedures could result in your governors being taken to an Industrial Tribunal for wrongful dismissal.

Whatever expedients may have been found, there have been many situations where redundancy has been unavoidable. In some cases, it has been the result of a falling number on roll and in some it has arisen from closure or amalgamation:

Q. I am a teacher-governor at an LEA Special School which the LEA proposes to close, along with another in the area. They plan to open a new Special School on our site. I know that the headship and deputy headship of the new school must be nationally advertised, but what happens to the teaching and nursery staff, of whom there will be a surplus from the two schools?

A. When the LEA goes ahead with its proposal, a shadow governing body should be set up to prepare for the opening of the new school and to appoint its staff. One presumes that this shadow body will be drawn initially from the two existing governing bodies and will be replaced by a normally constituted body once the new school has opened. It is for the LEA to arrange all this, although one would hope that they would seek the full cooperation of the existing governors.

It will be the duty of the shadow governing body to appoint the staff to the new school on an open and fair basis. One would hope that the LEA would have an agreed procedure for handling these delicate issues, including a statement of policy with regard to those teachers or support staff who do not secure a job. Such a procedure might include opportunities for early retirement and voluntary redundancy. One would expect these matters to have been discussed with the unions whose members are affected.

In the great majority of cases, it has simply been a matter of money: the school has been forced to reduce its staff in order to balance its budget. Governing bodies, facing the problem for the first time, were badly in need of expert guidance. Some received it from the local authority, not always totally reliably, and some grant-maintained schools purchased specialist personnel services, which were not always familiar with the educational world. They all needed to start with the basics:

Q. For financial reasons, we have to make a member of the teaching staff redundant next September. What are the basic procedures? What criteria can be used to select a teacher in a primary school? Can we choose the most expensive? Can we take account of the teacher's personal circumstances, for instance being a sole breadwinner? Can we choose the weakest teacher?

A. Questions like these are taxing many schools throughout the country. They need to be addressed very carefully indeed because there are many opportunities for error.

The first and most important piece of advice I can offer is to do absolutely nothing until you are quite clear about the entire procedure to be followed from start to finish. You are, after all, dealing with people's livelihoods and the decisions you are going to make are painful enough without making things worse by getting it wrong.

Step by step, the procedure is as follows:

1 Announce that there is to be a redundancy.
2 Publish the criteria which will be used in identifying the actual post or teacher.
3 Inform the unions represented in the school and be prepared to consider any representations which they may wish to make on the subject.
4 Invite applicants for voluntary redundancy.
5 In the event that no volunteer is forthcoming, identify the teacher to be declared redundant, using the criteria, and advise the teacher accordingly, indicating that he or she has a right of appeal.
6 If an appeal is lodged, arrange for the appeal to be heard and decided.
7 Inform the LEA of the decision, upon which the LEA must take action within 14 days.

Establishing the criteria is the key decision. They must be capable of complete objectivity in interpretation and this means that matters relating to competence cannot be included. There are ways of dealing with poor teachers, but this is not one of them. More than one criterion will probably be needed and a clear order of priority must be established and followed scrupulously until the point is reached where only one teacher can possibly be identified.

Most governors would wish to place delivery of the curriculum at the top of their list, but, where that does not provide a clear answer, as may well be the case in a primary school particularly, it is acceptable to use budgetary considerations if one wishes. The criterion most favoured by teachers' unions is LIFO – last in, first out – and this is certainly likely to produce a clear and objective answer when other criteria do not. I do not believe it would be easy to consider the personal circumstances of teachers, because this is likely to introduce an element of subjective judgement which could be contested.

It is also of vital importance that the governing body should remit the task of identifying and implementing the redundancy to a properly constituted sub-committee, leaving a sufficient number of governors completely uninvolved to enable an appeal panel to be formed, which should be at least as numerous as the sub-committee which takes the original decision.

For LEA schools, consultation with the LEA is essential at all stages, not least because it is the LEA which must pay statutory redundancy compensation to the unlucky teacher. The LEA may have a scheme of enhancement of pension which would help in securing a volunteer in the early stages. Lastly, if the redundant teacher wishes to challenge the decision before an Industrial Tribunal, alleging unfair dismissal, the governors will want the LEA to defend their decision, bear the costs of doing so and meet any award of compensation in the event of losing.

Getting the procedure right is essential, but it is not everything. The human dimension must not be lost in concentrating on the mechanics. The issue of redundancy can have a devastating effect on the morale of an entire staff, whether they are directly involved or not. This is not an argument for secrecy but a case for total openness right from the beginning. Good timing and sympathetic explanation are of the essence here, as is a caring and supportive approach to the unhappy victim and all those who work with him or her. Attention to the personal details, including follow-up after the deed has been done, are the mark of good management and this should include the fullest possible explanation of timings, compensation payments and opportunities for career counselling, if appropriate. It even extends to the small but significant points, such as not informing the teacher to be dismissed on a Friday afternoon. There is no good time, but experts reckon Thursday morning is near enough to a weekend break, but not so near as to deprive someone of the immediate comfort of their colleagues.

One of the perils of writing on issues of this sort is that there is always a lawyer out there, waiting to pounce on an error, and with evidence to back it up:

Q. You state that 'matters relating to competence cannot be included' in criteria for selection for redundancy. In the case of Williams v Compair Maxam Limited [1982] ICR 156, it was declared that 'efficiency at the job' was a criterion which was capable of being accepted. Would you alter your advice on the basis of this case?

A. No, I do not think I would, not because I wish to challenge your legal expertise, but because I think that such a course is fraught with danger.

In the school context, where criteria relating to the curriculum are likely to have priority, governors might find themselves having to choose between two or more teachers from the same curriculum area. If they choose competence as their criterion, they are faced with problems of measurement and assessment of competence which, in the relatively short time within which they have to come to a decision, they would find it impossible to resolve in a demonstrably objective manner. Those who would argue that the new system of appraisal would help overlook the fact that the knowledge that appraisal statements might be so used would destroy the purpose of the exercise and the confidence which teachers should have in it. In any case, a formal appraisal is likely to take place every two years for each individual teacher and so would be unlikely to be done at the right moment for a redundancy exercise.

I would also argue that redundancy is not the right vehicle for dealing with incompetence. If a teacher is indeed incompetent, the procedures of warning, support and counselling should be invoked and, if remedial action fails, dismissal on the grounds of incompetence should follow.

This argument underlined the importance of establishing good criteria for redundancy:

Q. Redundancy has become an issue at our school and we have heard much talk of 'LIFO' as a criterion for deciding who has to go. What is the legal position?

A. LIFO is, of course, the acronym for 'last in, first out' and it is a very familiar concept in industry, when the subject of redundancy is discussed.

The legal position is that, under Section 188 of the Employment Protection Act, an employer who is proposing to make any employees redundant must announce in advance, amongst other things, the proposed method of selecting the employees who may be dismissed. In order to avoid being taken to an Industrial Tribunal for unfair dismissal, the employer must ensure that the method of selection is fair and based upon criteria which have been applied equitably to all eligible employees.

In that context, LIFO is seen by some trade unions as a very helpful criterion, because it is entirely objective, relating, as it does, solely to the length of time a person has been in that employer's service. In the context of schools, however, it may well not be very practical. When a school is placed in the unhappy position of having to reduce staff, the first consideration is likely be the delivery of the curriculum and this is usually the first criterion to be listed. Other matters important to the running of the school, such as the pastoral system and the management structure, may well find a place on the list, leaving LIFO as a final criterion when all the others have been applied without arriving at the required number of potential redundancies.

It must be stressed that these are only examples: it is up to the employer to determine the criteria appropriate to the particular circumstances. The important requirements are to publish a list of criteria in the order in which they will be applied and be sure both that their application will lead to the identification of those who may be dismissed and that all the affected staff will be able to work out where they stand in relation to the process.

Delivering the curriculum has to be the first consideration in staffing a school, but this, taken by itself, can lead to complications when one looks at other responsibilities which teachers may hold in addition to their teaching duties. These may also need to be included in the selection criteria.

Q. I teach in a Special Unit for children with emotional and behavioural difficulties attached to a junior school. The governors have decided that they have to declare redundancies in the main school and have told me that I have to be considered with the rest of the staff, even though I hold a particular post. Is this correct?

A. Yes. When redundancies are declared, the entire workforce of the establishment has to be considered and, although you hold a special post, you cannot be excluded on that account.

It is the next stage which is more important from your point of view. The governors have to set out the criteria which they will use in determining which teachers shall be made redundant and they may well decide that the curriculum needs of the school come first. In that case, if you are the only person qualified and experienced to meet the curriculum needs of the pupils in the unit, you would probably be eliminated from consideration. If there is more than one person so qualified, other criteria may be applied, for example the cost of the post to the school budget, or the need to retain leadership skills, or whatever else is deemed appropriate. The criteria must be objective and must be fairly applied. You have a right of appeal, if you think you are being treated unfairly.

The right of appeal can be a source of difficulty to a governing body which is insufficiently aware of what it is about in such matters:

Q. Our school is having to make several teachers redundant. When a teacher appealed against a decision made by the governors' staffing committee, the appeals committee upheld the appeal because they did not believe in the policy of redundancy, which the full governing body had accepted. What on earth should we do?

A. It seems that some fairly direct governors' training is needed here. It is always painful when redundancy has to be faced and one can understand why some governors are upset by it. However, no committee of the governing body should challenge a policy decision which the full body has established. A decision to uphold an appeal against redundancy, which was not related to the substance of the individual case, is one on which the full governing body could intervene by instructing the committee to hear the case again, on the basis that it had not acted within its delegated remit, which should be to hear arguments on cases, not on the policy.

It may be necessary to review the committee structure to ensure that the remits are clearly stated. Those governors who are nominated to chair committees should be given appropriate briefing on their powers and functions before they tackle actual cases.

Redundancy is defined in law and means that either the position or the work is no longer required by the employer. This would appear to exclude Heads altogether from consideration, but does it?

Q. Our school has to reduce its teaching staff by three to meet its budget and redundancy seems the only answer. Can the Head be regarded as one of the three even though she has to be replaced, because we shall save quite a lot, her salary being protected at a higher level than the school's present group?

A. The case is well worth arguing, especially if, by making the saving on the Head's salary, you do not need to make a fourth teacher redundant. Obviously, a new Head will have to be appointed but the governors might postpone the appointment for at least a term, if they are confident that one of the existing Deputy Heads will prove a competent Acting Head. Although it will be necessary to pay several 'acting up' salaries, the total savings may well prove sufficient to balance the budget. Assuming your Head is willing to volunteer for redundancy, this should be an acceptable course of action.

Not surprisingly, the lawyer was quick to jump on this one:

Q. You claim a Head might be made redundant to overcome a budget problem. Surely, this cannot be the case, because there is no diminution of the work which has to be done?

A. You may very well be right, but my answer was concerned with a practical solution to a practical problem. It also had the advantage of leaving everyone concerned happy.

The Head was happy because she was enabled to take voluntary redundancy, which she very much wanted, three or four staff were happy because they had the prospect of an enhanced salary for up to two terms and the rest of the staff were happy because none of them had to be made compulsorily redundant. The governors and the LEA were pleased to be spared the embarrassment and difficulties attendant upon declaring a compulsory redundancy, while the governors had the additional satisfaction of having a balanced budget. One has to ask in whose interest it is in these circumstances, to challenge the legality of the proceedings.

You might also be wrong. It has always been the custom of LEAs to consider the teaching establishment of a school simply as an aggregate number of teachers, including the Head. We all know that the Head carries different responsibilities and duties, but this was ignored in such calculations. Therefore, if it is decided that the establishment must be reduced by one, it can just as well be the one who happens to be Head as any other.

It is important to remember that, in this instance, I am talking about a temporary arrangement and not a permanent one. The Head leaves and the governing body takes two terms to fill the vacancy with a new appointment, a time lag which is not uncommon when a Head's departure is announced at a fairly late date. In the interim period, the headship is filled by internal promotion to acting headship, so that the functions are actually carried out. The school operates during that period, which might well be until the end of the financial year, with its overall establishment reduced by one. By the time the next year begins, other staff changes, or a new budget, may have resolved the original problem. When a Head is willing to depart in this way, it seems unfair, to say the least, that he or she should not enjoy the same benefits as any other teacher who accepts voluntary redundancy.

Although I omitted to say so at the time, I actually knew of a case where that had happened.

For those who are made redundant, whether voluntarily or otherwise, there are other pitfalls to watch out for afterwards:

Q. In August, I was made redundant voluntarily with enhancement of my pension. My former school has now offered to employ me in a non-teaching capacity, but the LEA says that, if I accept the job, I shall have to forfeit the enhanced pension. Have they the right to do this?

A. While re-employment following redundancy is dealt with by law, the enhancement of pension is entirely at the discretion of the employer, who is entitled to set conditions when granting it.

If you look back at the papers which dealt with the offer of voluntary redundancy plus enhancement of pension, you will almost certainly discover that the LEA made it a condition of the offer that you would not enter their employment in any capacity for a term of years. In accepting the deal, you accepted the terms, which are now contractually binding upon you. So, if you do take the job, you will have to send the money back.

The following case was a particularly distressing one for the teacher involved and was an example of what can happen when governors do not seek appropriate advice before acting:

Q. Last year, I accepted a voluntary redundancy package from my college, which included an enhanced pension, a redundancy payment and salary in lieu of contractual notice. The County Council then declared that the terms I had been given were ultra vires and failed to pay the enhanced lump sum and enhanced pension. Do I have any right of redress?

A. It is quite possible that the terms which you were offered were outside the relevant regulations, but, nevertheless, they were offered to you by your employer, whom you had no reason to disbelieve, and you accepted them in good faith. You might argue with justification that, had the terms, as they now appear, been offered, you would not have accepted them, not least because your calculations about your future financial position have been substantially altered.

I recommend strongly that you take legal advice on this issue. If you belong to a union, I hope that they would be prepared to take on your case, for which there are a number of precedents where courts have awarded compensatory damages.

One particular trap to avoid is, in certain circumstances, taking up a new job immediately after losing the old one:

Q. If a teacher is made redundant, can he or she take up an appointment elsewhere immediately without forfeiting the right to the redundancy payment?

A. This is a complicated issue and anyone finding themselves in this situation should take personal advice relating to their particular circumstances.

In general terms, teachers benefit from the Burgundy Book agreement that service with any LEA is counted as continuous when moving from one LEA to another. This is important in protecting employment rights, such as sick-pay, maternity leave and security of employment. For someone facing redundancy, this carries the important benefit that all LEA service is taken into account when entitlement to compensation is calculated.

Taking up another post with an LEA immediately following redundancy, where the offer of the post has been made and accepted before the date of the redundancy, may disqualify one from receiving the redundancy compensation, on the grounds that the employment is continuous. This is the roundabout which balances the swings, but it does not apply if a gap of over four weeks intervenes between one job and the next or where the new post does not recognize continuity of service from the last one.

It is important to note that this restriction can extend well beyond teaching jobs:

Q. Further to your answer about entitlement to redundancy payments, does the rule about loss of rights apply where the redundant employee moves immediately to a post outside teaching?

A. Yes, it does. I am sorry that I failed to mention in my previous answer the key regulation on redundancy in this context which is the Redundancy Payments (Local Government) (Modification) Order 1983, SI 1160 (1983).

This Order covered a wide variety of public service employers, ranging from the fire service to local authority rating valuation panels. Apart from teachers and other local government employees, it included other bodies such as the Commission for the New Towns, Housing Corporations and the like. It was modified in 1989 to include, among others, grant-maintained schools and CTCs.

The effect of the Order is to deny the right to redundancy payments to an employee of any of the listed employers who takes up a new post with the same or any other listed employer within a period of four weeks after the date of the redundancy. Where the offer of the new job is made after the end of the old contract, the rule does not apply. What is important is the timing of the offer and the starting date of the new job – and it makes no difference whether it is part- or full-time.

Any teacher facing redundancy must therefore be very careful when looking for subsequent employment and be sure that, if the new job starts straight away, the new employer, if in the public service, is not included in the extensive list made under the 1983 Order and its 1989 supplement.

8

Heads and governors

Since the reforms of 1986 and 1988, which shifted power away from local education authorities and onto school governing bodies, the lines of demarcation between the powers, duties and functions of governors and Heads have been the focus of much argument. Whether in grant-maintained schools or in those still under the now looser structure of LEA control with delegated management, the distinction between policy making and the day-to-day management of the school has come under the spotlight, but never been precisely defined.

Some people have sought to produce a definition, while others have suggested that such an attempt might well prove counter-productive. The truth is that, in the great majority of schools, Heads and governors have worked out together a style and a practice which works perfectly well for them, with the minimum of friction and the maximum of cooperation in what is, and should be, a partnership designed to serve the best interests of the school and its pupils. This has produced not one model of how the relationship should be managed but a range of models, each working happily for those engaged in them.

At the same time, tensions do arise, as my postbag has shown, and, in a small minority of schools, these tensions have led to a complete breakdown in the relationship, which has inevitably been damaging to the schools concerned and brought a premature end to the careers of their Heads. Not all cases have been so catastrophic and the less serious incidents have indicated the need for a voluntary Code of Practice which would provide both governors and Heads with guidelines to the best way of conducting their relationship. This should be supplemented by model Standing Orders, which governing bodies might wish to adopt in order to give them a procedural framework within which it would be easier for them to deal with another problem which has come up in correspondence, the 'rogue' governor, who will not accept the views of the majority, or behaves in a manner which they find unacceptable.

One correspondent thought he had found a novel way to get rid of an unsatisfactory governor:

Q. When a local authority appoints governors to a school, is it under a duty of care, particularly when reappointing governors to a governing body whose previous performance, especially in financial matters, had been shown to be seriously at fault?

A. I do not believe that a local authority is under any duty in this matter, other than to comply with the law requiring them to nominate persons who are qualified in law to serve.

The failures of a governing body are collective, not individual. Individual governors have no powers of their own, unless they have been specifically delegated by the whole body. The governors nominated by the local authority are only a minority of the total membership and are, as a group, no less and no more culpable than the rest.

Thus, if the performance of the governing body has been at fault, only the governing body can be accountable for it.

The local authority, which is responsible for the oversight of all the schools under its control, has only one effective sanction, the withdrawal of delegated powers, taking the responsibility for the direction of the school back into its own hands.

What you are really asking is whether there is any way of ensuring that those whom local authorities nominate to serve as governors are competent to do the job. The answer is no – and there is no way of ensuring that other governors, whether elected by parents or teachers or co-opted by the governors themselves, are competent either.

The Head's task, unlike that of the governors, is legally defined. The *School Teachers' Pay and Conditions of Service Document* states that the Head is responsible for 'the internal management and control of the school'. But where does internal management end and policy begin? The following question illustrates the point and also, incidentally, shows how the Head may be able to fudge the distinction to serve his or her own ends:

Q. Who should decide on the year group structure and numbers within each class? The governing body of this school is adamant that Year 6 pupils should not be grouped vertically with Year 5. As a result, we have two very small classes in Year 6 and a reception class of 30.

A. The allocation of pupils and teachers to classes is part of the internal organization and management of the school and, as such, falls clearly within the duties of the Head. One would expect, therefore, that the Head would arrange this as he or she sees fit and keep the governing body informed of the situation.

The Head is, however, subject to any policy decisions which the governing body might choose to make and it could be argued that a policy of not mixing age groups could be laid down by them as part of the framework within which the Head has to work.

In practice, however, one would expect a responsible governing body to be guided by the Head in what is essentially a matter of professional judgement. As a well-seasoned sceptic, I have to say that it crossed my mind that your Head may actually be responsible for this policy and is using the approval of the governing body to avoid a direct confrontation with you. If so, it is sad, because important issues of this sort ought to be openly discussed by all the staff, even if the ultimate decisions may not please everybody.

It may be, of course, that well-meaning governors simply want to become more closely involved. A proper distinction of roles should, however, be maintained:

Q. Does a governor have the right to attend staff meetings?

A. The organization of staff meetings is part of the internal management of the school and thus a direct responsibility of the Head. It is for the Head to determine if and when such meetings shall be held, bearing in mind that he or she has a duty to consult, what the agenda should be and who should be present. No one else has any right in the matter.

The governing body, however, as the employer, or effective employer in LEA-maintained schools, has the power to act collectively to summon a meeting of its employees for its own purposes and to determine who should be present thereat. The agenda for such a meeting should not, however, include matters which are the proper responsibility of the Head.

In practice, such legal niceties should be unnecessary, provided that governors are properly aware of their role and good relationships exist between them and the Head.

It is particularly tempting for individual governors to be drawn into matters affecting individual pupils, especially when they are lobbied by parents. Succumbing to that temptation may well bring a governor into conflict with the Head:

Q. One of the governors of this school is seeking to interfere in decisions I am taking with regard to the discipline of pupils. Is this legal?

A. The problem of the over-zealous governor crops up quite frequently and requires diplomatic handling. While you wish to maintain a proper separation of the function of governors from that of the Head, you might well find it counter-productive to make an enemy of an individual governor, who may think that he or she is trying to help somebody, even if it is not you.

Dealing with the legal point first, it is quite clear in the statement of the Headteachers' Conditions of Employment that the internal management and control of the school is the province of the Head. That includes the administration of pupil discipline, although the governing body has the right, if it chooses to exercise it, to lay down the principles upon which discipline in the school should be based. The Head is, in any case, accountable to the governing body for the manner in which his or her duties are carried out, but this is an accountability to the governors as a whole and not to any individual governor.

It follows, then, that this governor is in the wrong to interfere in individual cases, not least because he or she would be prejudiced if a decision of yours, for example on exclusion, should become the subject of appeal to the governors at a later stage. It may be that a tactful explanation of the respective roles of Heads and governors in the process is all that is needed here, but, if the problem is persistent, you should seek the support of the Chairman of the Governors to explain the position.

Similarly, governors may try to tackle issues relating to individual members of the staff, which also fall within the Head's responsibilities:

Q. A member of the governing body recently took it upon himself to reprimand a teacher who, he alleged, was not teaching effectively. What should I, as Head, do about this?

A. I think that you should object to this behaviour with a strength which reflects the actual gravity of the offence.

The internal management of the school is entirely the responsibility of the Head and that includes the direction and, if need be, the discipline of the staff. Interference by an individual governor is intolerable.

What one does about it will depend very much upon circumstances and personalities. If this governor has behaved impulsively or in ignorance, then it will be necessary to explain quietly to him the impropriety of his conduct and suggest that it should not be repeated. The best person to do this is likely to be the Chairman of the Governors who would be able to indicate that there are ways and means of drawing attention to the supposed inadequacies of a member of the teaching staff which are appropriate and which will be taken seriously.

One would hope that this would suffice but, if the behaviour persists, it might be necessary for the governing body as a whole to be made aware of it and to express formally its disapproval of the misconduct of one of their number. The LEA has powers to remove an LEA nominated governor whose conduct is entirely disruptive and out of order. It is important to remember, however, that this kind of action relates to improper behaviour, not to awkwardness, 'bloody-mindedness' or just plain obstructive opposition. For that kind of behaviour only political tactics may be used.

Sometimes, the issue is even more clear-cut, as this example shows:

Q. Two parent-governors at this GM school have been coming into school and attempting to control the movement of pupils around the building, complaining that some of our practices are unsafe. What are their rights in this matter?

A. This appears to be a case where the governors have not properly understood their role or their powers. Their actions are unacceptable.

The first point to make to them is that individual governors have no rights or powers as individuals, other than those which the full governing body sees fit to delegate to them. They have no more right to act in the way they are doing than any member of the general public and, if they are there without the Head's permission, he or she would be justified in asking them to leave.

The second point is that the general control of the building and the movement of pupils around it is specifically the responsibility of the Head, who is charged with the internal management and control of the school. In exercising this responsibility, the Head is subject to any policy statements or directions which the governing body may wish to make.

There is a fine line to be drawn, however, between interfering busybodies and legitimately concerned parents and this example may repay closer examination. The trick in matters of this sort is to convert what is an unacceptable excess of zeal into productive and supportive concern. It is not always possible, but the attempt to do so should always come before angry confrontation.

Assuming that some governors are worried, rightly or wrongly, about the health and safety of pupils using certain parts of the building, it would be in order for the governing body to set up a committee to investigate and report. It would be sensible to discuss the issue with the Head and to involve the school's Safety Officer in the investigation. Agreement should be secured in advance about how the investigation should be conducted and, if observation of pupil movement was to be included, times and places should be arranged with the Head. There should be no question of the governors attempting to direct or control pupils.

The outcome may be that the worried parents are reassured. It is also possible that they may notice problems which the school, through familiarity, had not spotted and so bring about useful improvements.

Operations of this nature serve to promote a proper partnership between governors and professionals, in which both come to a better appreciation of their respective roles.

As this response makes clear, good person-management skills are always likely to produce better results than boundary confrontations.

Governors may also be tempted to use their position for other purposes, no doubt for the best possible motives:

Q. As IT Coordinator in a GM primary school, I am being put under pressure by some of the governors to purchase computers for classroom use which I and my colleagues believe to be unsuitable for our purposes. They are not prepared to consider either what is already in use or our advice. I accept that they are my employers, but is their conduct acceptable?

A. No, it is not. First, these particular governors are not your employers: you are employed by the whole governing body, acting collectively, and individual governors, or groups of them, have only such powers as the full body has explicitly delegated to them.

Second, these governors are stepping well beyond the ill-defined line which separates the powers and duties of governors from those of the Head. It is the duty of the governing body to set the budget and within it they will allocate specific sums for the purchase and maintenance of equipment, including computers. Decisions about the spending of that budget fall within the internal management and control of the school, which is vested in the Head. He or she is accountable to the governors for spending that money efficiently and effectively in the interests of pupils and, if the governors feel that this has not been done, they have the duty to say so.

One would not expect a Head to leave decisions on the purchase of equipment to governors, nor should governors seek to arrogate this to themselves. On the other hand, if there are governors who have specialist knowledge of computers, the Head would naturally wish to consult them before coming to a decision. In the end, governors should rely upon professional expertise in matters which relate, as this does, to classroom practice.

There are, however, occasions when the governors, exercising their undoubted powers, come into conflict with the Head and with the teaching staff:

Q. *My staff are 'up in arms' because the governors have reinstated a very disruptive boy, against my advice, following a permanent exclusion. Do they, or I, have any right of appeal against this appalling decision? What happens if the staff refuse to teach him?*

A. An order to reinstate made by the governing body is final: there is no appeal and the school has no alternative but to comply.

You describe the decision as appalling but one must presume that there was some reason behind what seems to you and to your staff such a perverse decision. I suggest that you discuss the implications of this case and disciplinary procedures in general with the Chairman and propose that the Disciplinary Committee should have a meeting with staff representatives in order to achieve a better level of mutual understanding. Governors do not always appreciate the full impact which disruptive pupils have in a school, but teachers do not always understand the external considerations which may influence governors when they deal with individual cases.

One thing must be clear, however. It is not open to the governing body to reverse the decision once taken, unless it was based upon a degree of misinformation which would warrant a rehearing. Simply to change their minds as a result of staff pressure would give the parents a straightforward case of a breach of natural justice.

You and your staff must, therefore, accept the decision with as much grace as you can muster. There is nothing to prevent you imposing a strict 'contract' of good behaviour upon this boy and excluding him again if he breaks it. A refusal to teach him would, however, be a breach of contract on the part of the teacher and would only exacerbate the situation.

There are a few instances where the law actually enters the field and lays down how the relationship should work. The case of non-teaching staff is one such:

Q. Can a governing body dismiss a non-teaching employee without the consent of the Head?

A. Yes, but they cannot act without considering the Head's advice. Schedule 3 of the Education Reform Act 1988, which deals with the powers of governing bodies under LMS, lays down that the Head and the Chief Education Officer have the right to be present at all proceedings of the governing body relating to any dismissal and that the governing body must consider their advice.

To consider advice does not mean that it must be accepted – and it is, of course, conceivable that the advice received could be conflicting – but it does mean that it must actually be discussed. The fact that it had been considered would appear in the record of the meeting, together with the reasons for its rejection, if it was so decided. To act against professional advice in a matter of this kind would be hazardous, because the Chief Education Officer might be in a position to say that any costs consequent upon the dismissal might fall on the school budget. To ignore the Head's advice might demonstrate a lack of confidence in him or her, which would seriously damage the trust which should exist between the Head and the governors.

Demarcation between lay governors and the professionals is further complicated by the fact that they are entangled by the system itself. Teachers elect their own representatives to sit as governors and the Head may be a governor *ex officio*. Should the Head accept that position?

Q. I have just been appointed to my first headship. Should I become a governor of the school or not?

A. That is for you to decide, and it is a genuinely free choice, with arguments on both sides.

Those who would advise you not to become a governor believe that the Head's role should be that of a chief executive officer, charged with the duty of giving professional guidance and advice to the governing body and carrying out their policy decisions. They argue that the Head should not become involved in the making of those policy decisions, because it compromises his or her position as the impartial servant of the governing body.

On the other side, it is contended that the Head is not prevented from acting in a professional manner by joining the governing body. He or she has no need to take sides in contentious issues and might indeed be well advised not to do so. The fact of membership, however, gives the Head a seat at the table, which cannot be denied. Only when items are being discussed which involve the Head personally is he or she obliged to declare an interest and withdraw.

Heads who are governors also feel that, as the teaching staff is represented by its elected representatives, they too should be there as of right. They also point out that there are some key decisions, for example co-option of governors and votes on grant-maintained status, when the decision is taken by ballot, so that the Head can cast a vote, which may be crucial, without openly declaring an opinion.

My personal view, for what it is worth, is that you should become a governor. The majority of Heads have done so, believing that the advantages outweigh the disadvantages. The minority view is, however, strongly and sincerely held and, in practice, it may not make much difference. Far more important is the establishment of a good working relationship, based upon mutual respect and understanding of the respective roles.

None the less, a governor is a governor is a governor:

Q. As a headteacher who has opted to be a governor, can I vote on co-options and count towards the necessary quorum? The DFEE School Governors' Guide to the Law refers to 'elected and appointed governors' and I am neither.

A. Certainly you can. The headteacher is a governor '*ex officio*', that is by virtue of the office which he or she holds, and is, therefore, appointed as a governor in that capacity.

If the Head does decide to become a member of the governing body, the questions do not stop there:

Q. My LEA advises me, as a newly appointed Head, not to serve as a member of the committees of the governing body, but simply to attend as a professional adviser. Do you agree?

A. There are arguments both ways on this, but my preference has always been to recommend Heads to participate as full members.

If you are a member of the full body, there is little logic in taking a stand-off position on the committees. If matters affecting you personally were to be discussed, you would have to withdraw in any case.

Apart from that, the fact that you are a member means that you cannot be excluded from the meetings in any other circumstances, and this may be valuable. On the other hand, even though you are a full member, you are not obliged to use your vote on every occasion and you might choose to adopt a professional position and abstain on matters of political controversy, where you did not wish to compromise your position with either faction.

It should not be inferred from this that the Head is in a position to decide which committees to attend as a member, although there is always the fall-back position of professional adviser:

Q. Our governing body has stated in its pay policy that no governor who is employed at the school may be a member of the Staffing and Pay Committee. Have they the right to do this?

A. Yes. Governing bodies may establish committees with whatever membership and terms of reference they choose, although certain regulations have to be observed in particular cases. For example, no teacher-governor may be appointed to chair a committee.

Employees are not automatically barred from sitting on the committee which deals with staffing issues, although they would, of course, be expected to declare an interest and withdraw if any matter affecting their own position was being discussed. Some governing bodies welcome the general advice which employees can give to such committees, while others, like yours, decide that they would prefer to exclude them.

Q. We have received a request to include one of the teacher-governors on the staffing committee of the governing body of this rather small grant-maintained school. Would this create conflict of interest in dealing with grievances, discipline and redundancy issues, especially if the teacher-governor is a union representative, and also in discussions affecting the pay of individuals or groups of staff?

A. This is a matter which the governing body must determine for itself, but it must start from the premise that all governors are equal, with teacher-governors having exactly the same rights and duties as the rest, with the sole exception that teacher-governors are not allowed to take the chair, either of the full body or a committee thereof.

The question of interest is often misunderstood. When used in this context, it refers to a direct personal interest, which is usually financial, in the matter under discussion. When such an interest exists, the person concerned should declare it and withdraw completely from the discussion. When the interest is general, there is no need for such a withdrawal. It only becomes necessary when the interest of the individual is greater than that of the generality of those concerned.

To illustrate this, using the examples you quote, let us suppose the committee is discussing redundancy. In dealing with the general question of whether there should be any redundancy at all, the teacher-governor's interest is no greater than that of the entire staff. If the decision reached affects the teacher-governor's own subject area, then he or she does have an interest and must withdraw. In handling a disciplinary case, if the hearing might result in the dismissal of a teacher, for whose post the teacher-governor might be an applicant, then an interest exists (or might be said by others to exist and be prejudicial), and a withdrawal is indicated. Similarly, in considering pay, if a decision is one from which a teacher-governor may benefit by more than the generality of teachers in the school, then he or she should not take part.

These limitations are far from being a disqualification and it could be argued that the knowledge and experience of the teacher-governor and the awareness of staff opinion which he or she brings to the governing body are particularly relevant and helpful to the work of a staffing committee.

The fact that a teacher-governor is also a union representative is irrelevant. This teacher is elected by the staff, not union members, and sits as a governor with all the rights and duties of that office. If he or she behaves simply as a union representative in that context, the Chairman would be entitled to point out that it is inappropriate.

Teacher-governors occupy a special position because of their dual role and other governors are sometimes a little wary of them, as this question showed:

Q. One of our governors has sent a letter to the school staff relating to business under consideration by the governing body, without the knowledge of her fellow governors. As she is a teacher-governor, we are concerned about the effect this will have on future discussions. Should she have done this? How could the governing body prevent this happening again?

A. I am not sure that there is anything to be concerned about here. It is entirely natural that a teacher-governor, even though she is not actually a delegated representative, should wish to consult her colleagues on the staff on matters upon which she may have to take decisions on the governing body. It is, after all, more valuable to the governing body if she can convey the general view and not just her own opinion.

The only exception to this would be if the governing body had passed a resolution to classify a particular item of business as confidential. In those circumstances, she would have been out of order in discussing the matter, whether orally or in writing, outside the meeting. The governors actually have no legal sanction to prevent this happening, but one would hope that a firm word from the Chairman would be sufficient to remind her to respect the normal conventions.

The business of declaring an interest needs further elaboration, which is given in the next two answers, the first of which also deals with a dreadful procedural confusion. Both the Head, as professional adviser, and the Clerk to the Governors must take a share of blame for allowing this situation to develop:

Q. Is it proper or lawful for a Personnel Sub-committee to discuss and propose to the full governing body salary increases for the Head and Deputies, 'subject to funds being available', without prior reference to the Finance Committee? Should the Head withdraw from the Finance Committee when it considers how to pay for the increases?

A. What a mess! I certainly would not have started from here.

In the first place, the Personnel Committee should have full delegated powers in the matter of determining staff salaries and not be proposing changes to the full governing body.

In the second place, the Personnel Committee should be operating within an agreed pay policy, upon which all their decisions should be based, and within a budget for the total salary bill previously delegated to them. They should certainly not be in the position of proposing increases without knowing whether or not they can be paid for.

In the third place, no individual, neither the Head nor anyone else, should be a party to the discussion of matters in which they have a direct personal interest.

This governing body needs to sort out its structure and procedures as a matter of urgency. There is little that is proper in the situation you describe and very great scope for all sorts of difficulties.

The Chair of Governors made a similar error in the following case and, once again, proper procedures had been neglected:

Q. The Chairman of Governors at our school, acting on the advice of the Head, told the teacher-governors to leave the meeting when the pay of the Head and Deputies was discussed. Had she the right to do this and had the Head the right to tender such advice?

A. There are a number of things wrong here.

First of all, the full governing body should not have been discussing this matter. It is the business of the governing body to adopt a pay policy, which is then implemented by a committee, duly constituted for that purpose. If the full body debates the details, there is no impartial group of governors left to whom a teacher may take a complaint or grievance about a decision on pay.

Whether teacher-governors should be members of the committee set up for this purpose is a matter for the governors to decide. There is no rule which makes them ineligible and they are as much entitled to take part as any other governor. The only circumstances when they should not take part is where they have an interest. An interest, in these circumstances, is defined as a direct personal one, that is, where their own financial position, or that of someone closely related to them, is under consideration. A teacher-governor should only withdraw when his or her interest is greater than that of the generality of teachers in the school. Thus, they could take part in a discussion on the general pay policy of the school, but not in one related to specific allowances which they held, or to which they might aspire.

There is in this nothing which indicates that they should withdraw from a discussion of the pay of the Head or Deputies, in which they are not directly concerned. The Head, in the case you cite, tendered incorrect advice and the Chairman was wrong in accepting it.

Both governing bodies and Heads need to be aware not only of procedures but also of the limitations imposed on their freedom of action by statute and by local authority regulation. The Articles of Government form the constitution within which a governing body must operate and the following letter, on an issue which is happily now only of historical interest, brings this out:

Q. In the controversy over Key Stage 3 English testing, some people have argued that, if the governors instruct the Head and staff not to administer the tests, they are taking responsibility for the decision. Do you agree?

A. No. Governing bodies are set up under statute and their powers and duties are set out in Articles of Government. Nowhere are they given the authority to set aside the law of the land, which is effectively what is being considered here.

The tests in question are imposed by regulations made under statutory authority and are therefore mandatory upon those who are charged with the duty of administering them. A governing body which sought to instruct teachers to do otherwise would be acting outside its powers, *ultra vires*.

It would be the duty of the Head and of the Chief Education Officer (if the school is maintained by an LEA), as professional advisers, to point this out to the governors.

A Head or teachers who acted upon an instruction which they knew at the time to be *ultra vires* would not exempt themselves from responsibility for their action.

Whatever the legal position, however, the expression of opinion by the governors on this important matter gives significant support to staff who feel strongly about these tests. Willingness to stand up against a law which is judged to be silly or pernicious has a long and respectable history, but those who do it need to be aware that that is what they are doing.

The local authority position was raised by the following:

Q. The governors of this LEA school wish to change the duties of the caretaker, but he insists they have no right to do this unilaterally. Can he obstruct us in this way?

A. I am afraid he can. Most LEA employees, from teachers to office staff, enjoy conditions of service which were established, often many years ago, as a result of agreements reached between the employers and trade unions. These conditions form part of contracts of employment.

When governing bodies, under local management of schools, took over much of the responsibility for employing their own staff, they were obliged to accept and to honour those previous agreements, except where the services in question became subject to compulsory competitive tendering. While cleaning services were privatized, this did not extend to caretakers, who have remained directly employed.

Contracts can, of course, be changed, but this can only be done effectively by agreement and no caretaker is likely to want to negotiate for less favourable terms than he or she currently enjoys. Equally, few governing bodies want to get involved in the business of collective negotiation with unions, because they do not have the experience or the professional backup to do so effectively.

In practice, Heads have found that, whether they are in LEA or grant-maintained schools, the business of guiding, informing, persuading and attending their governing bodies and all their committees is a very demanding part of their job:

Q. Am I, as Head, required to attend meetings of the governing body, including their committees, whenever they choose to hold them?

A. One has to make a distinction here between the position of the Head as a governor and as the person charged with the management of the school.

As a governor, the Head has the same rights and duties as any other, but could be disqualified for failing to attend any meeting within a six-month period. Not all Heads choose to exercise their right to be a governor and this requirement does not, therefore, apply to them.

However, the Head also has professional duties in this area and these are specified in the *School Teachers' Pay and Conditions of Service Document*, where Section 30(16) states that the Head has the professional duty of:

> *'... advising and assisting the governing body in the exercise of its functions, including (without prejudice to any rights he may have as a governor of the school) attending meetings of the governing body and making such reports to it in connection with the discharge of his functions as it may properly require either on a regular basis or from time to time.'*

One must conclude from this that the Head is very much subject to the governors' pleasure in this area and the only defence which a hard-pressed individual might be able to advance would be that the requests which were being made of him or her were unreasonable.

All of which makes a strong case for the operation of senior management teams in schools, with the workload shared between the Head and a group of senior staff, enjoying full mutual confidence and working effectively together.

9

Appointments

It is not surprising that appointments of teachers and, even more, Heads and Deputies, should figure high amongst those issues which set staffrooms by the ears. Schools are close communities and there are few changes of personnel which do not make a significant impact within those communities. As a result, anything related to promotions or to new appointments from outside excites lively interest and speculation. This is especially true of internal appointments, where there will always be arguments about whether they should be subject to external competition, advertised only within the school or simply dealt with by the Head or a committee of governors.

Making internal appointments without even the appearance of open competition can cause the most bitter resentments, even amongst those who know they stood no chance of getting the job anyway.

Q. Is it acceptable to advertise a senior teacher post only within the school and can we limit applications to those who already hold specified levels of responsibility?

A. The only posts which must by law be advertised nationally are those for Head and Deputy Head. It is, therefore, quite possible to advertise internally and to consider only internal applicants.

You may make whatever specification you choose about eligibility to apply, but I would question the wisdom of doing so. There may be teachers who have not yet reached the level you think is appropriate, but who might actually be excellent candidates. More significantly, they may entertain ambitions for promotion and deserve the chance to 'set out their stall', even though they are not appointed. To exclude them without consideration may well cause unnecessary frustration and resentment.

The law in this matter can also be frustrating, especially when governors think they know what they want before they start:

Q. We have a vacancy for a Deputy Head. One of the senior teachers, who serves on the management team, is outstanding and already does the job effectively. Can we promote him to the vacant post without all the bother of advertising and interviews?

A. No. The regulations require that all appointments to headship or deputy headship must be nationally advertised and the set procedure for making the appointment must be followed.

Having said that, the regulations do not say how many applicants have to be invited for interview, nor when the advertisement has to be placed. I do not recommend that you place the advertisement in an uninformative style in the middle of the holidays and then invite only one applicant for interview, but, if that is what your governing body decided to do, they would not be breaking the law.

What I would advise them to do is to advertise the post honestly and openly, draw up a short list, interview in their usual manner and appoint the person who is manifestly the best candidate. If your senior teacher is as good as you believe, then he will get the job, and feel all the better for having done so in fair and open competition. If he does not, neither he nor anyone else will have cause to feel aggrieved and the good reputation of the governing body will be maintained.

When seeking to make new appointments, it is important to take into account those who are already employed, because there might be problems ahead:

Q. We have employed a temporary teacher for two years, but we are now advertising to fill the post permanently. Are there any problems if the temporary teacher does not get the job?

A. Indeed there are. By serving for two years continuously, your temporary teacher will secure full rights under employment legislation. If the job goes to someone else, your governors are highly likely to face an action before an Industrial Tribunal for wrongful dismissal and with no defence to offer. They certainly cannot make the temporary teacher redundant, because there is a continuing demand for the work. An urgent rethink is needed here.

Q. We have a part-time teacher of long standing, working four-fifths of full time. We now need a full-time person for this subject and the part-time person is unwilling to take this on. Can we terminate her contract and then appoint the full-timer we need?

A. This is not an appropriate case for redundancy, because there is a continuing need for the work which this teacher is doing. If the teacher has been in continuous service for more than two years, she enjoys full employment protection under employment law and could take your governors to an Industrial Tribunal for wrongful dismissal, with every prospect of success. Even if the contract has been annually renewed, continuity of service will provide her with the protection of the law.

If negotiation does not succeed, you will probably have to meet your additional demand with another part-time appointment.

There is always the worry that one might make a bad appointment, and this can be a particular problem at a senior level. Some people have tried to find a way round this difficulty:

Q. Can I appoint a Deputy Head on a renewable contract of, say, three to five years?

A. There is nothing to stop you doing this except the possible reluctance of teachers to apply for the job. When the Borough of Solihull tried some years ago to adopt this approach in respect of a junior school headship, the idea did not prove popular and, although the post was filled, the idea was dropped.

The general point is that teachers' pay scales take into account the fact that security of tenure is normally very high. If short-term contracts are introduced, it would be reasonable to expect salaries to be higher in order to compensate for the lack of security. If you are able to pitch your salary offer at an attractive level, you may find that you have applicants of good calibre; if not, you may be disappointed.

The wording of the advertisement is an important matter, not just for attracting the desired applicants. One must take care not to infringe the law on equal opportunities, in respect of race or gender, or to discriminate against the disabled. These things are not always immediately obvious:

Q. Some advertisements, such as those for Heads and Deputies, quote an age requirement of less than 45. This appears to be an infringement of the Equal Opportunities legislation, since women, who have taken time out for family responsibilities, probably up to five years, would find it harder to acquire the necessary experience by that age. What is your opinion?

A. My opinion is as good as the next man's, or next woman's come to that, and it does not really matter. What matters would be the decision of a court in a directly relevant test case and, to the best of my knowledge, no such case has been brought.

In general terms, I think it unwise to make such a stipulation in an advertisement, not because of legislation but because it is an unnecessary restriction on good applicants of both sexes. It is also unwise to look exclusively at experience, in terms of total years of service, in appointing senior staff. Qualities of vision, imagination and leadership are even more important, and these can be present and evident whether an applicant has a continuous record of service or not.

Applicants for jobs are required to give names of persons to whom reference may be made. My postbag shows that this is a fertile field for speculation, worry and discontent, mostly because the subject of the reference does not see what has been written.

Q. I have been unsuccessful in finding a teaching post, having just returned from a year's travelling abroad. At my last interview, the Chair of Governors hinted strongly that the reference from my last headteacher was 'extremely uncomplimentary'. What rights do I have to ask to see this reference, as it is obviously having a detrimental effect on my chances of employment?

A. Unless the headteacher concerned works for an employer who insists that all references must be made available to their subjects, you will have no rights at all in this matter.

When you filled in your application form, you were probably asked to provide details of people to whom reference might be made. Confidentiality may, or may not, have been specified, but this makes no difference, if the reference has been sought in confidence. It was, incidentally, a breach of that confidentiality for the Chair of Governors to reveal the nature of the reference, even if it was helpful for you to know about it.

It is your responsibility, as the applicant, to ascertain whether a referee is willing to support your applications and you should ask permission to use someone's name before doing so. This provides an opportunity for the referee to warn you, if the terms of the reference will not be wholly favourable, giving you the chance to go elsewhere, if you wish.

If you have been given to understand that you would be given a supportive reference, you should write to your referee about the apparent discrepancy and you may judge from the reply whether you should continue to use that referee.

Q. There is a real concern amongst staff at this school that many staff references are being taken up without leading to interviews. Do teachers have the right to see references written by the Head?

A. The subject of confidential references has always been controversial and some LEAs have adopted a policy that all references must be open, that is, accessible to those about whom they are written. In most cases, however, they are written under the seal of confidentiality and teachers do not have the right to see them.

The trouble with references is that those who write them are often reluctant to disclose the fact that they cannot offer total support to the applicant, because they have no wish to demoralize them in their current job. Such a view is mistaken, because it leads directly to the kind of suspicions which prompted your letter.

Good management practice should ensure that, whether a teacher sees the actual document or not, he or she should be well aware of the general nature of its contents. A teacher's intention to apply for a post elsewhere should be discussed in advance with the Head, who should indicate whether he or she believes the application to be realistic or not and whether he or she is prepared to support the application with a positive reference. Such a discussion should include consideration of the strengths and weaknesses of the teacher and, if the Head intends to refer to any of the latter in a reference, that should be made clear at this stage.

Clearly, this is not happening in your school. You need not assume, however, that the Head is necessarily writing unfavourable references. It is common practice in many schools to take up references on many candidates, often prior to completing a 'long list', let alone a 'short list', and your colleagues may just be unlucky so far.

The best way to seek the reassurance you need is for the matter to be raised with the Head in general terms, perhaps by the union representatives in the school. Without the need for quoting specific instances, they might try to persuade the Head to adopt a more open approach so that the current mistrust may be dispelled. If the school has a Professional Tutor, with a particular responsibility for staff development, he or she might be the appropriate person to talk to the Head.

An aggrieved individual may also tackle the issue directly by asking the Head to discuss the nature of the reference, although without necessarily seeing it. A Head who wishes to reassure a teacher, but does not want to create a precedent by showing the actual document, might agree to show it, in confidence, to a third party, for example a union representative or teacher-governor, who would then be in a position to confirm that it gave positive support.

Many people hope and expect that the introduction of a professional system of appraisal will put an end to worries about references, because it is reasonable to suppose that the appraisal statement will be the principal source upon which references are based.

A useful protection for those on whom references are written – provided they know about them – has been offered by the courts:

Q. Does a teacher have any redress, if a Head supplies a reference which is false or unfair?

A. Possibly. In an important judgement given in the House of Lords in 1994, it was held that an employer had a duty of care in providing a reference. The case (Spring v Guardian Assurance and others), which had nothing to do with teaching, concerned an employee in the insurance industry who was given a reference, which the trial court judge had described as 'so strikingly bad as to amount to ... the "kiss of death" to his career'. The plaintiff was able to establish that there were serious inaccuracies in the reference and the House of Lords held that he was entitled to rely on the employer to exercise due care in its preparation, because of the special knowledge gained in the employer–employee relationship.

This judgment should not be interpreted to mean that any unfavourable reference is open to challenge, but it is a warning to all employers who write references that they must exercise due care to ensure that whatever they write is truthful and capable of substantiation.

Even when the subject of the reference has seen it, for instance in those schools where a policy of open references is applied, there still remains the lingering suspicion that something else may be said over the telephone:

Q. Can you tell me if a reference has to be in writing and is there any redress against an inaccurate oral reference? Is there a time limit on seeking redress?

A. In my view, a reference should always be given in writing. The practice of giving oral comments is open to abuse and arouses suspicion and mistrust. Having said that, I have no doubt that the courts, if presented with a case, would hold that the duty of care with regard to accuracy would apply, although there would clearly be a much greater difficulty in establishing the facts.

There is no limit on seeking redress, but common sense would suggest that a very long delay might make it more difficult to collect the evidence.

The question of what goes into a reference and what does not exercises the minds of both subject and writer:

Q. Is there any remedy available to a teacher who has been made redundant, once the period for lodging a claim for unfair dismissal has elapsed? Should the fact of contesting one's dismissal damage one's prospects of a favourable reference?

A. Unless there were circumstances surrounding the redundancy which might give you a claim for damages in the civil court, I can see no remedy to your situation. If you are a member of a union, you should refer the facts of your case to them as soon as possible: if there is anything which can be done, they will certainly be able to advise you.

On the matter of a reference, I do not believe that a school would feel vindictive simply because a person had fought hard to keep a job. Your departure was related neither to incompetence nor to misconduct and, unless you have firm evidence to believe otherwise, you should assume that your previous employer will provide a fair appraisal of your service.

Q. I have a very good teacher on my staff who went through a very difficult period a little while ago because of a serious problem with alcohol. There is no sign of the problem now. The teacher is now applying for promotion elsewhere and I am not sure how to deal with the matter, particularly if I am asked a direct question about health.

A. There are two clear duties which should guide you in this, the duty of honesty to the school seeking the reference and the duty of openness to the teacher concerned.

If we view alcoholism, as we should, as an illness, we can honestly respond to an enquiry about health by saying that the teacher went through a period of poor health, but now appears to be well. This gives the recipients of the reference the opportunity, if they wish to take it, of asking the applicant at interview or informally beforehand for additional information. This places the responsibility where it properly belongs, with the teacher.

In this, as in all matters related to references, where there is not an open system, it is good practice to discuss the contents of a reference with the teacher concerned. In this instance, you can reveal precisely what you intend to say about the illness and add that, should the potential employer seek clarification, you would be obliged to give it.

If the request for a reference says nothing about health, you have then to determine whether the seriousness of the problem at the time was such as to warrant your mentioning it anyway. In most cases, I suspect that one would, not least because the recipient would have cause for grievance if, having appointed the teacher, the problem recurred almost immediately.

Failure by a referee to provide full information can have serious consequences for those on the receiving end. The old rule of *caveat emptor* applies to references as well as to shoddy goods.

Q. A teacher whom I appointed last year has had an appalling record of attendance. I have discovered that this was also the case in his previous appointment, but no mention of this was made in a reference which I received from his previous employer. Do I have any redress against the referee?

A. Although you may seek information and guidance from a variety of sources, the responsibility for making the appointment is yours. As far as the reference is concerned, you should remember that the referee is under no obligation to mention matters which are against the subject's interest, unless requested to answer specific questions. If your letter seeking the reference made particular mention of health or attendance record and you were told that this was good, then you have every reason to be aggrieved. If the question was not asked, or if, having been asked, it was not answered, the blame lies with you for not spotting and acting upon the omission.

If you have reason to believe that the referee deliberately lied, your first move should be to write to seek an explanation. If you are not satisfied, you should complain formally to the referee's employer.

Unfortunately, this gives you no immediate remedy against the subject of the reference, unless he too can be shown to have lied deliberately in response to a direct question. If he did, you may have grounds for terminating his contract.

There are occasions when people would be glad to be spared the duty of writing a reference and there are occasions when a reference is refused.

Q. Can a Director of Education refuse to supply a reference for an applicant for a headship?

A. Nobody can be compelled to provide a reference for anyone, but it is the normal expectation that senior officers, be they Heads or Chief Education Officers, will do so for those who have served under them, unless there are specific reasons for refusing.

It has long been the practice with regard to headships in LEA-controlled schools that the opinion of the Chief Education Officer should be sought and accorded due weight. If, therefore, a reference is being refused, an explanation should be sought at once. If necessary, a professional association or union might be asked to intervene.

This response provoked an immediate challenge from the barrack-room:

Q. *You said that no one can be compelled to provide a reference. Are not headteachers bound by their conditions of service to provide 'information about the work and performance of the staff employed at the school where this is relevant to their future employment'?*

A. Although I am not aware of the matter having been tested in a court, I believe that there is a clear distinction to be drawn between providing information and writing a confidential reference.

You are quite right that the *School Teachers' Pay and Conditions of Service Document* imposes the duty to provide information, but this can be provided in an open document, available to the person about whom it is written. A Head could, it seems to me, satisfy the requirement by writing something on the lines of, 'Mr A has been employed at this school as a teacher of B since 19xx. He has taught classes from Years X to Y and his performance has been generally satisfactory.' Such a bald statement would offer little to a potential employer and do nothing to enhance the chances of the applicant.

On the other hand, where a prospective employer asks specific questions, a Head should answer them honestly, although, even here, these answers could be confined to matters of record relating to work and performance, and need not be written in confidence.

A Head is entitled to inform a teacher who asks for a reference that only such information as is on the teacher's file will be provided and that it will not be written in confidence.

Questions of eligibility for appointment are not common, but one correspondent raised the question of religion:

Q. I was interested to read that, under Section 30 of the 1944 Education Act, a religion, or lack of it, cannot be a disqualification for employment in a state school. Yet, I have seen advertisements explicitly asking for a religious qualification in the TES. As an atheist, I have always thought this to be a human rights issue. What exactly is the situation?

A. It is as you have stated it in your question, but there are two possible explanations for the advertisements you have seen, neither of which contradicts the central point.

The first is that Section 30 does not apply to church voluntary-aided or voluntary-controlled schools, where the governors may make adherence to the particular faith of the school a condition of employment. This is often the case, particularly for headships and, even where it is not a requirement, teachers may be contractually obliged to respect the religious basis of the school.

The second is that you may have confused religious qualification with religious belief. If a school is seeking to appoint a teacher of religious studies, they may well consider it appropriate to specify a qualification in theology or in the teaching of religious studies and they may explore the teacher's competence in these matters at interview, without inquiring at all into his or her personal faith. It is perfectly possible to have an atheist teaching religious studies, where the governors are satisfied that he or she is competent to do so.

The actual process of appointment can also be a source of trouble, largely because it is conducted necessarily behind closed doors in a situation where there is usually only one winner and several potentially disgruntled losers. In independent and grant-maintained schools, the appointment of teaching staff is often left entirely to the Head, who may, or may not, involve governors in the process. In LEA schools, governors are more frequently involved. The regulations allow a fair amount of discretion in this, but they are much more specific when it comes to appointing Heads and Deputies.

Q. Our school is about to appoint a new Head. Who actually makes the appointment, the interviewing panel or the governing body?

A. Regulation 25 of The Education (School Government) Regulations 1989, (SI 1989/1503), as amended in 1991 (SI 1991/2845), prevents a governing body from delegating the function of appointing a Head or Deputy Head.

They may, however, set up a panel to manage the process, but the panel's decision must be in the form of a recommendation which the full governing body must ratify. The regulations also specify what must be done if the governors disagree.

Some people simply cannot resist getting involved, even when they ought to retire to a safe distance!

Q. Our Head, who is retiring at the end of this term, is a member of the panel set up by the governors to appoint her successor. Is this allowed?

A. I can quite understand that the governors feel the need for professional advice in making such an important appointment and it is natural, if not necessarily wise, that they should turn to the professional person they know best.

The law provides only limited guidance. The Education (School Government) Regulations 1989, (SI 1503), lay down that a Head, acting as a governor, cannot vote on the appointment of her successor nor, unless the governors specifically permit it, can she participate in the discussion.

This does not prevent the governors nominating the Head to the appointing panel, although this does seem to contradict the spirit of the law.

The outgoing Head clearly does have important knowledge and experience about the school's needs which should be part of the broader range of considerations affecting the governors' choice of a successor, but they should have the courage to seek additional support, whether from the LEA or a specialist consultancy, in coming to their decision.

As for the Head, I should advise her to decline the invitation. However wise and experienced she is, her view is bound to be coloured by her own personality and experience and, particularly if she has been long in post, by her commitment and emotional ties to her school. Even the best-run schools need sometimes to change direction and, if the Head is too closely involved in the appointment of her successor, the long-term interests of the school may not be served.

Another contentious issue is whether the teachers at the school should be involved in the appointment of the Head.

Q. The junior school where I teach has amalgamated with an infants' school on the same site. The Heads of both schools have applied for the headship of the new school. Is it normal for teacher-governors to be excluded from the whole procedure of advertising, interviewing and selecting?

A. It is hard to define 'normal' in such a situation. I would rather apply the test of reasonableness.

The first presumption with teacher-governors is that they should be treated in exactly the same way as other governors, unless there are specific reasons why they should be treated differently. If, for example, a teacher-governor might be in a position to gain promotion or an incentive allowance as a consequence of a particular appointment to the headship, then this might be construed as a personal interest which would disqualify him or her from taking part.

In the particular case which you cite, it is for the interim governing body which is managing the amalgamation to establish the interviewing panel for the headship. They may well have considered, or been so advised by the LEA, that the feelings among the staff of the two schools about this appointment are very strong and that, therefore, the appearance of genuine impartiality and fairness might best be preserved by excluding the teacher-governors from the formal process. This they have the undoubted right to do.

Having said all that, I am bound to add that I believe that a sensitive and well-managed appointing process should have built-in opportunities for the views of the staff to be known. This may be done by informal discussions with the Chairman on the general view which the staff take of the needs of the school and of the kind of person with whom they would feel happiest to work. There is much to be said also for the staff to have the opportunity of meeting all the candidates called for interview for sufficient time to form at least some opinion about them and for any such views to be made available informally to the Chairman.

The appointing panel has no need to act upon these views but they form part of the background against which the eventual decision is made.

There are many views about how an interview should be conducted, not least because there is the need to treat every applicant fairly and equally. This may cause as many problems as it solves:

Q. As a governor, I am worried about the interviewing style adopted by the Head in making internal appointments. Candidates were interviewed by the school management team, plus one governor, each of whom asked set questions prepared by the Head. The result caused some upset in the staffroom, with resentment against the members of the management team. Do you regard this as a satisfactory method?

A. It is for the governing body itself to determine how it wishes to handle making appointments and it is a matter to which very careful consideration should be given.

Some governors feel that it should largely be delegated to the Head, because he or she is better qualified to make professional judgements, but this is to understate the potential contribution which lay governors can make. They are very often able to offer fresh insights on candidates, as well as upon the needs of the school, which add an important dimension to professional assessment.

Internal appointments are always the most difficult, because one has to live with the disappointed applicants afterwards. It is particularly important to ensure that every candidate is made to feel that the procedure has been fair and open, whatever the outcome, and that he or she has had a proper opportunity to present a case.

The procedure which you have described seems to me to be faulty on at least two counts. Firstly, the dominance of the management team in this instance is likely to lead the unsuccessful candidates to believe that the 'favourite' was chosen, because there was, with the exception of the one governor, no one present who was not involved in the day-to-day running of the school. Secondly, the very formal approach adopted, with only set questions asked, may leave interviewees with the feeling that they were not given an opportunity to develop particular strengths or interests.

Some people think that asking all the applicants identical questions is the only way to ensure equal opportunities for all. I am not convinced of this, although great care must be taken not to allow such a disparity of approach that any candidate is given an unfair advantage.

Lastly, I am not against the involvement of the school management team in the selection process. It is common and good practice to include a specialist, for example the relevant Head of Department, in the final interview. I do not favour using the whole team in the final process, however, because this may be too inward-looking. There is much to be said for a two-stage approach, with the team taking part in preliminary interviews, with their views conveyed to the final appointing panel for information.

There are some things, however, which should not be asked at all:

Q. Can we ask candidates for teaching posts if they are married and whether they have children?

A. In most circumstances, such questions are entirely irrelevant to the interview and they ought not to be asked. In certain instances, for example in boarding schools, it would be relevant to establish the family situation for certain posts.

The reason for not asking them is not simply because they are irrelevant but because, if a candidate was led to believe that the answers to those questions influenced the eventual decision, there might be a case to answer under the Equal Opportunities legislation.

Having managed to get safely past the interview stage, there are still hazards ahead when it comes to making the decision:

Q. Our governing body has recently begun the process of appointing a new Head and is endeavouring to adhere to the correct procedure. In the event of their not wishing to appoint any of the candidates whom they short-list, do they have to start the process again from the beginning or can they choose a second selection from amongst the existing applicants?

A. There are no specific rules governing the numbers on the short list and governors are free to interview any applicants they wish at any stage. It is often the case that narrowing a long list down to five or six for interview cuts out candidates who are well worth seeing and a second scrutiny of those discarded first time round may well prove fruitful.

Governing bodies in independent or state schools may appoint consultants to assist them with the process of appointment, but LEA schools are more likely to depend for professional guidance on the Chief Education Officer, or his representative.

Q. Under LMS, are we obliged to act upon the advice of the County Education Officer when we appoint a Deputy Head?

A. No. The Chief Education Officer is entitled to attend all proceedings, including interviews, relating to staff appointments for the purpose of giving advice. When the appointment is for headship or deputy headship, he or she has the duty to offer such advice as he or she considers appropriate.

It is the duty of the governing body, or its interviewing panel, to consider that advice, although they are not obliged to act upon it. Commonly, the Chief Education Officer's advice would not be to appoint a specific candidate but rather to indicate to the panel which candidates were professionally judged to be the most competent. Upon occasions, the CEO might feel constrained to advise that a particular candidate was unsuitable for appointment. In all cases, one would expect the governors to attach due weight to the advice given, even when it is not finally taken, but, where the CEO advises **against** appointment, it would be unwise to ignore it, because the governors would be fully liable for any untoward consequences if the CEO were proved to be justified.

My comments on the appointment of Heads produced two curious questions, which simply would not have occurred to me to ask:

Q. Now that governing bodies are responsible for the appointment of Heads, is it possible that an unqualified teacher could be appointed in a maintained school?

A. I don't think so. The question of the employment of unqualified teachers is dealt with in the Education (Teachers) Regulations, 1989, where it is laid down, in Section 13, that:

> *'Save in the cases specified in Schedules 3 and 4 and subject to regulations 15, 16, 17 and 18, no person shall be employed as a teacher at a school unless he is a qualified teacher.'*

Regulations 15–18 refer to teachers of hearing and visually impaired pupils and Schedule 3 refers to unqualified nursery teachers employed before 1989 and to student teachers. Schedule 4 refers to instructors who are not qualified teachers, who have 'special qualifications or experience', who satisfy the relevant body as to their qualifications and/or experience and may be appointed if 'no suitable qualified teacher or licensed teacher is available for appointment'. Where such an appointment is made, it must only be 'for such period as no suitable qualified teacher or licensed teacher is available'.

In relating these regulations to the position of headteacher, we must take note of Section 6 (2)(a) of the same document, which states that 'the staff of teachers employed at a school shall include a headteacher'. From this it is clear that the law regards a headteacher as a kind of teacher and so the rules with regard to qualification apply.

Given the fact that the law also requires all vacancies for headship to be advertised, it is hard to conceive of circumstances in which no suitable qualified teacher was available to fill a headship. If an unqualified candidate were preferred to a qualified teacher, and if the unsuccessful person appealed to the Secretary of State, it would be difficult to persuade him that the governing body was acting reasonably.

Q. Is it legally possible to have job-sharing in the post of headteacher?

A. The concept of job-sharing has no foundation in law: it is an example of good employment practice which provides opportunities, most commonly for women with young children, for people to take jobs which would not otherwise be open to them. In reality, job-sharing is simply the division of one post into two part-time appointments in an arrangement where the two employees, who may or may not divide the work equally, work together to ensure that the full requirements of the position are delivered. It is for the employer to determine whether a particular post is capable of being filled in this way and there is no legal compulsion upon him to do so. Each case should be decided on its merits.

The concept has been applied with apparent success to teaching posts in schools, where it is for the Head or governors, as the case may be, to decide whether to accept it. I know of no instance where it has been applied to headship and I do not believe that it would be acceptable. The post of headteacher is the only one specifically required by regulation (Education (Teachers) Regulations, 1989) and this refers to it in the singular. The legal responsibilities of headship are not, in my view, capable of being shared, even if the resultant confusion in the minds of teachers, parents and pupils could be overcome.

After the post has been filled, there remains the not unimportant consideration, from the applicants' point of view, of expenses:

Q. As an LMS school, are we required to pay travel and subsistence expenses to those we invite for interviews for teaching posts?

A. Assuming the LEA has delegated this item in your LMS scheme, it is for the governors to determine their policy in this matter, although they may be guided by the LEA in doing so. I suspect that any school which failed to meet the out-of-pocket expenses of candidates for jobs would very soon run out of applicants.

It is hard to imagine a more foolish or misguided approach than is suggested by this question. It is in the best interests of any school to get the best possible applicants for their teaching posts and one would expect every effort to be made to persuade candidates that the school was welcoming, positive and generous in its dealings with potential as well as actual staff. Even unsuccessful applicants can carry away good or bad impressions which are conveyed to others and may affect the school's image.

Money spent on attracting and securing good teachers is money wisely invested. Parsimony here could do untold damage.

Q. I was interviewed unsuccessfully for a teaching post and, although I was invited to apply for my travelling expenses, in spite of repeated reminders from me, these have never been paid. Do I have any rights in this matter?

A. If the school promised to pay travelling expenses, you attended interview on that understanding and have a right to expect your claim to be met. If they still have not paid you, try lodging a claim through the Small Claims Court. This is easy, cheap and often effective.

Lastly, because people do lodge complaints about appointments for all kinds of reasons:

Q. What records should be made at the time an appointment is made?

A. It is very important that all those concerned with making appointments should be aware of their responsibilities and of the fact that their decisions may be challenged under legislation relating to race relations and equal opportunities.

If an unsuccessful applicant chooses to take a complaint before a tribunal, any documents relating to the process of appointment, even including notes which may have been made by the interviewing panel at the time, may be required by the tribunal and used as evidence. It is, of course, easy to say that the person who seemed to the panel to be best qualified or most suitable was appointed but it is much better to be able to produce a record made at the time which makes it quite clear how it was decided. This is particularly important where there is any possibility that an applicant might argue that the decision was prejudiced on grounds of sex, race or colour.

It should therefore be the normal practice to preserve all application forms and related documents and to make a note at the time of the appointment of the criteria which were used by the appointing body in reaching their decision. It is also good practice to advise members of the appointing panel in advance of their responsibilities, of the criteria and of the need to avoid questions which might lead a candidate to infer the existence of prejudice.

10

Admission of pupils

Once upon a time, the admission of pupils to state schools was a simple matter and rarely the cause of dispute. For the great majority, the school one went to was the one in the area where one lived. There were particular arrangements for denominational schools and, in a few areas, there remained the possibility of passing an entry test for a grammar school.

The Education Reform Act 1988 changed all that by introducing the concept of parental choice and stopping local authorities allocating pupils to schools simply on the basis of catchment areas. For the great majority, choice was a misnomer: at best parents were able to express a preference which was by no means always satisfied, but that preference was something which could not be totally ignored.

Q. The local authority is directing our school to accept more pupils than we can, in our view, accommodate and more than our Standard Number as originally agreed. Can the governors refuse to accept them?

A. Responsibility for admissions to all LEA-maintained schools is vested in the local authority and the concept of the Standard Number was written into the Education Reform Act 1988 in order to prevent local authorities rationing admissions to popular schools in order to sustain numbers in others. It would appear, in your case, that the policy has been too successful!

Section 26(4) of the Act does allow the local authority to fix the number of admissions for any age group at a higher level than the Standard Number, but Section 33 of the Act requires the local authority to consult the governing body at least once every school year as to whether the arrangements are satisfactory and also to consult the governing body before varying those arrangements.

If there has been no consultation, the governors have good cause for complaint, although I doubt whether they will ultimately succeed in preventing the extra admissions. An application to the Secretary of State, on the grounds that the local authority is acting unreasonably in the exercise of its powers, might at least have a nuisance value in obliging the authority to justify its actions.

Q. How is a school's Standard Number for admissions calculated?

A. This was very precisely laid down in Section 27 of the Education Reform Act 1988. The language of the act is too abstruse to reproduce here, but the gist of it is that the Standard Number refers to the number in the relevant age group, either in 1979, or, if the school was opened after that date, the number established at the opening. Changes in existing Standard Numbers can only be made by the Secretary of State and the Act lays down the process for seeking such changes.

The choice of 1979 was not accidental: in national terms, that year saw the highest level of admissions during the period preceding the passage of the 1988 Act. Thus, popular schools were given the maximum opportunity to expand.

As the chapter on Exclusions also shows, the powers of local education authorities over admissions to schools under their control have been a regular source of dispute, although, to be fair to them, the law allows them very little flexibility in the face of expressed parental preference, when places actually exist in the chosen school.

Q. What is the validity of an admission number laid down by the LEA? May it be varied by governors or the LEA? What relevance does this have for class sizes? Can the LEA insist that children should be admitted to places in classes outside their normal year group, against the wishes of the governing body?

A. There are two strands running through this question which need to be separated: admissions and school organization.

Admissions are the responsibility of the LEA and, while they should consult with the governing body in deciding their policy on admissions, they have the right to direct the school to admit pupils. The governors should certainly bring pressure to bear on the LEA if they believe that the number of admissions is causing difficult educational or staffing problems, but, given the importance attached to parental choice, LEAs are likely to prefer to vary admission numbers rather than to try to put up barriers.

The way in which pupils are allocated to classes once they are admitted is part of the internal management of the school, which is entirely the responsibility of the Head. So it is not the LEA which insists that children are placed outside their normal group but the Head who decides to solve the problem in that particular way. On practical grounds, there may be no alternative solution, but, if this is a recurring problem in the school, it might be worthwhile for the Head and staff to review their organization to see whether a better system might be devised.

One of the early challenges to the Education Reform Act related to the question of local authority boundaries. Prior to the Act, LEAs had been able to insist that children who lived within their area should attend their schools. Arrangements were occasionally made for crossing the borders, but they were usually resisted. In urban areas particularly, this became a contentious issue and it was taken to the High Court by the London Borough of Greenwich.

Q. We are an oversubscribed primary school near the LEA boundary. Following the Greenwich decision, we are obliged to accept children from the neighbouring authority, who walk past their local school to get to us, in preference to children from the area in our own authority which used to be our priority catchment zone. Our LEA allows other schools not adjacent to the boundary to have priority areas, so why can't we?

A. The answer is contained in the Greenwich decision which you mention, which laid down that parental preference cannot be denied simply because they are on the 'wrong' side of a boundary.

It is for the LEA to determine the admission policy for all its schools and, by making distance from the school a criterion for priority, it can effectively establish an area from which most of a popular school's children will come. What it cannot do, as a result of the court judgement, is to make exceptions, in applying that or any other criterion, to children who live outside their area.

The governors of your school could make representations to the LEA, asking for a change in the admissions policy, but there is no change which could legally be made which could alter the Greenwich ruling.

The Education Reform Act did not cover preschool education and this caused problems for at least one school:

Q. My LEA has a policy of admitting children to a nursery school on the basis of social priority from within a designated catchment area. As a result, the school cannot always offer places to children from within the area who do not meet the criteria. As the nursery school is linked to the infants' school, this has an effect on enrolment there. Can this policy be challenged?

A. As nursery schooling is not compulsory, the LEA is entitled to establish its own criteria for admissions and the law relating to parental choice does not apply. It does apply, however, in the case of the infants' school, where, I imagine, the LEA operates a different policy.

Your problem is that, having failed to secure a place at the nursery school, parents may take their children elsewhere at the infant school stage. They do not have to do so and it is up to the Head and governors of the school to ensure that parents are made aware that there are places available for their children, regardless of their earlier rejection.

The denominational schools continue to enjoy a special position in regard to admissions, although their freedom to reject pupils is limited:

Q. I read somewhere that church schools can reject pupils they do not want. Is this true?

A. It is not quite as simple as that. A judgement in the Court of Appeal overruled an earlier High Court decision which had denied to church schools the right to refuse entry to pupils who were not Christians. The Appeal Court's ruling was that a church school could refuse to admit pupils, even when there were spare places, on the grounds that to admit them would affect the character of the school as one dedicated to a particular faith.

This decision means, therefore, that the governors of church schools can refuse to admit pupils, but only on the grounds which were argued in this case.

Most schools are happy to admit as many pupils as they can find room for, not least because each pupil brings a useful addition to the school's budget. There are occasions, however, when they are far from happy:

Q. Our LEA is insisting that we accept onto our roll a pupil who has a long record of serious disruption and is the subject of a Statement of Special Educational Need. Neither I, as Head, nor the governors want him. What are our rights?

A. The control of admissions to LEA-maintained schools is vested in the LEA, but they are limited in the exercise of their powers by the right of parents to choose the school they want for their children and by the law governing Standard Numbers for admission.

What this means in practice is that, provided that there is a place at your school within the Standard Number, the LEA can insist that you accept the parent's choice and admit this pupil. Good LEA practice would be to engage in the fullest possible consultation about the case, involving the parents where appropriate, with a view to trying to resolve the issue by agreement rather than compulsion. In the last resort, however, the LEA has a statutory duty to provide every child within its area with full-time education and it may direct you to admit him.

The question of the Statement is relevant, in that Part 3 of the Statement specifies the nature of the support which is required to meet the needs of the pupil, as identified in Part 2. The LEA has the duty to ensure that the support is provided and that may mean additional resources for that purpose. Governors should insist that this is done.

Of course, the fact that you must admit a pupil does not confer a duty to keep him. If his behaviour continues to be seriously disruptive, he should be subject to the normal discipline of the school, including, if necessary, exclusion. Here again, the LEA has the power to order reinstatement, albeit with a right of appeal on the part of the governors.

Cases of this sort appear to be on the increase, a reflection of a policy of closing LEA special units and the incorporation of pupils with special needs within the mainstream. While there may be good arguments for the policies behind these trends, the system of formula funding is not geared to providing the level of resources needed to manage the more difficult problems. Furthermore, in a period when governing bodies seem to be more concerned with examination results and a favourable public image, their willingness to adopt a tolerant and patient approach to pupils with special needs is likely to be limited.

In a competitive environment, with grant-maintained schools and voluntary-aided as well as independent schools controlling their own admissions, many problems can be caused as a result of the timing of the admissions process. An agreed local timetable, to which all concerned are prepared to adhere, is the ideal solution, but this is not always achieved.

Q. We are having great difficulty in establishing our admission list for next September, largely because of the inefficiency of the LEA. Can the governors take over responsibility for the procedure?

A. The governing bodies of grant-maintained and voluntary-aided schools have responsibility for admissions. In LEA-controlled schools, the control of admissions is vested in the LEA by law and the governors, while they may offer their advice and make their protests, are bound to accept the LEA's decisions.

LEA control extends also to the process employed in determining the allocation of pupils, according to statutory requirements and any local rules which they have drawn up. In areas where these matters are contentious, there is bound to be a certain amount of delay in settling final lists, because of the need to allow for appeals procedures. Unless it can be shown that the LEA is breaking the rules or acting unreasonably in other respects, your governors must simply be patient.

Parental choice, or preference, is not absolute, mainly because the legislation refers throughout to 'the relevant age group'. Attempts to bypass that may not succeed:

Q. A parent recently asked if we would accept a child into our comprehensive school one year ahead of the normal age of transfer, because he had 'completed the national curriculum' at the primary school. If we have room, must the parent's wishes be complied with?

A. No. Control over admissions into LEA-maintained schools is entirely vested in the LEA. If they refuse this request, the parent has a right of appeal, but I think it would be unlikely to succeed. Even an appeal to the Secretary of State that the LEA's policy was unreasonable would, in my view, be uncertain of success, unless, perhaps, the parents could demonstrate convincingly that the LEA was totally failing in its duty to provide an education for this pupil appropriate to his or her age, ability and educational needs and that the only way in which these requirements could be met would be by admission to a secondary school.

Because sixth-form education is outside the statutory requirement, some people have assumed that the rules governing admissions did not apply after the age of 16. The following questions explored various aspects of this.

Q. Who controls admissions to the sixth form? This school follows a policy of open access, but do we have the right to refuse anyone?

A. You do not mention the status of your school. If it is grant-maintained, the admissions policy is laid down by the governors and agreed by the Secretary of State. If it is an LEA school, admissions are controlled by the authority.

In either case, it is unlikely that the policy for the sixth form will be different from the rest of the school, although it could be. For pupils who were in the school in Year 11, the question does not arise anyway, because they are already on the roll and may continue if they choose to do so. To refuse them entry to the sixth form, unless there is a policy in place that imposes an entry qualification, would be the equivalent of exclusion.

For new students entering from outside, the same criteria apply as for admissions lower down the school: if there are places available, parental choice must be respected.

Q. Our LEA is seeking to impose the admission to the sixth form of a boy who did very badly at GCSE, whose whole attitude to school was poor and for whom we can offer no appropriate course. Surely, as he is over sixteen, we don't have to take him?

A. Ridiculous though it may seem, the law says that you do. The Education Reform Act 1988 made no distinction with regard to age when dealing with admissions. Control over admissions to county schools is vested in the LEA, subject only to the limit of the Standard Number for any year group, as defined in the Act. It is highly unlikely that the Standard Number would ever apply to the sixth form and the only other limit which the LEA might impose is one of the physical accommodation. In this, too, they will set their own figure.

The only recourse which a governing body could have in such a case would be an appeal to the Secretary of State, under Section 68 of the Education Act 1944, on the grounds that the LEA was exercising its powers unreasonably. That would seem rather an unwieldy sledgehammer for this particular nut. I am inclined to think that the best policy would be to admit him and then, if his conduct does not indicate that he has been down the Damascus road since you last dealt with him, to use the normal disciplinary procedures, including, if need be, exclusion.

Q. My son expected to join the sixth form of his voluntary-aided school last September, having achieved an 'A' and several 'D's in GCSE. On the first day of term, the Head told him that there was no place for him at the school and that he should seek a place elsewhere. Did the Head have the right to do this?

A. Voluntary-aided schools, unlike county schools, usually have some control over their own admissions policy and may, therefore, establish criteria for membership of their sixth form. One would expect these criteria to be published in the school prospectus or elsewhere, so that pupils and parents should know what the conditions are.

If your son had satisfied such criteria, the school should not have refused him a place because, as he was already enrolled in the school, the refusal would have constituted an exclusion, against which there would have been the right of appeal to the governing body. I can only assume that this school has an admissions policy for its sixth form, based upon GCSE grades, which your son did not meet. In my view, it was very wrong of the school not to make this policy clear in advance.

Unwanted sixth-formers are one thing, adding to their number by whatever means is another. Many schools with sixth forms are envious of Further Education Colleges, who can recruit students of all ages. The next two questions indicate the opportunities and the drawbacks:

Q. Our school wishes to allow adults to attend sixth-form classes and to charge them fees for their courses. Can the staff refuse to teach them?

A. One would hope that a policy on admitting adults would be one which was arrived at as a result of consultation and agreement with the staff concerned. Presumably this is not so in your case.

Lacking other guidance, one falls back upon the statement in the *School Teacher's Pay and Conditions of Service Document* that a teacher is required to work 'under the reasonable direction of the Head'. Now, whether it is reasonable or not for you to direct your teachers to teach classes augmented by the inclusion of some mature students may depend upon a number of factors, such as the numbers of school and adult students involved, the extra facilities to be provided and the additional work created for the teachers.

The Head can, therefore, direct the teachers to accept the additional students and they, if they do not like it, can invoke the grievance procedure in order to convince the governing body and, where appropriate, an appeal committee that the direction is unreasonable.

All that is very formal and one would hope that you would be in a position to demonstrate to the teachers concerned that there were real benefits to the school, in which their subject areas would share, arising from the fee income which was being generated. It is hardly likely to be sufficient to allow the governing body scope to enhance salaries, although there is nothing wrong with that idea in principle.

Q. If we admit adults to our sixth-form courses, are we entitled to a capitation grant for them?

A. No. There is no prohibition on recruiting adults to classes in school, but you will not receive funds for doing so, either from an LEA or from the Funding Agency. You are, however, able to charge such students an appropriate fee.

Lastly, there is the problem of the pupil who has been admitted, but does not attend. Apart from a proper concern for the individual pupil, this did not trouble schools too much in the past, but with unauthorized absence figures now a matter of public report, schools would dearly like to do something about these intractable cases:

Q. We have a pupil who has attended for only 20 sessions over the past two years. The LEA has provided some home tuition, but has not brought a prosecution against the parents. Can we remove her from the roll?

A. The only reasons for removing a pupil's name from the roll are:

- Confirmed permanent exclusion
- Notice of withdrawal from parents
- Notice that she is enrolled elsewhere
- Instruction by the LEA
- Death

You appear to have none of these. Although I understand the effect this situation has on your attendance returns and the frustration you must feel, you cannot justify removing her in the present circumstances.

11

Examinations

In many ways, the work of secondary schools revolves around public examinations, the assessments of pupils' performance which take place mainly from the age of 16 onwards. The ultimate aim of most pupils is to enter the examinations and the results not only play a major part in determining career destinations but also, because they are published, affect the school's reputation. It is not surprising, therefore, that issues relating to public examinations have regularly appeared in the Helpline column.

Problems begin even before the examination stage is reached, because parents are anxious that their children have the best possible opportunities to shine. The constraints of the school's resources and its timetable may make it impossible to meet every demand.

Q. *We have pupil and parent demand for a GCSE course which cannot be accommodated within the existing timetable. Can this be taught outside the normal teaching time and can I direct teachers to undertake it, provided I do not increase their overall workload?*

A. In principle, there is nothing to prevent you adopting the course of action you propose, but there are a number of practical difficulties which you need to take into account.

The first essential is to consider the pupils. You may not be proposing to increase the teachers' workload, but are you going to increase theirs? Are they going to be taking this subject in addition to all the others and, if so, will they be able to cope? They may be showing enthusiasm now, but will this be sustained, with a longer school day and extra work, as the examination pressure begins to build?

As far as the teachers are concerned, if you are dealing with willing volunteers, you have no real problem, although the question of the length of their working day and the effect this addition may have on their performance needs to be considered.

If you are proposing to direct the unwilling in this matter, there is no immediate legal obstacle, providing that the overall requirement of directed time does not exceed 1265 hours. However, your teachers may contend that what you are directing them to do is unreasonable, in terms of the *School Teachers' Pay and Conditions of Service Document*.

If it can be shown that they are being deprived of 'a break of reasonable length' at midday, then it is, by definition, unreasonable. If the classes are to be held after or before school, the question of reasonableness might have to be tested by a grievance hearing, where the principal argument would presumably relate to the overall length of the working day, or perhaps to the fact that certain teachers were being required to accept conditions which were significantly different from those of their colleagues.

I do not say that the teachers would necessarily win their case, but I cannot imagine that the ill-feeling which it would generate would be very good for the well-being of the school, whatever the outcome. Issues like this are almost always better resolved by negotiation.

With pressure for success being felt by parents, pupils and teachers, there is a temptation to think that extra work could make all the difference.

Q. One of my staff has offered to give her examination class additional teaching outside normal school hours. Can the governors agree to this and should they pay her for doing it?

A. A teacher who takes up work outside contractual duties and hours may do so voluntarily or under a separate contract. Many teachers engage in evening class work on this basis and are paid at whatever the agreed rates are for such service. Whether the students get this service free or pay fees is also a matter for agreement.

I should, however, advise caution before you decide to accept this proposition or recommend it to your governors.

Consider for a moment the message which is being conveyed to the parents. The implication is that there is insufficient teaching time for this subject on the timetable, so that the students will only obtain good grades if they enrol for this extra provision. What does that say about the school? Is that really the message you wish parents to receive?

Alternatively, is this teacher saying that she is such a poor manager of her teaching programme that she cannot cover all the work in time which is adequate for everyone else? Is that what she wants parents to think?

What about her colleagues? Are they going to be worried that the pressure and extra time which this teacher is imposing on the students will have an adverse effect on their performance in their subjects?

And lastly, what about the students? They may well feel under pressure to take on this extra commitment, but is this a burden they ought to have to bear? Are the demands of school and homework at this stage of their careers not already quite enough?

I know that many parents seek additional coaching or evening classes for their children in subjects where they are weak and sometimes teachers will recommend this, or even provide it privately. These are matters of personal judgement and they can be beneficial in some circumstances. I am not at all sure that a school would be wise to become involved officially.

In some matters, it is possible for the school to be helpful:

Q. A parent has asked the school if we will enter his son for the GCSE in Serbo-Croat, the family's native language. Should we agree?

A. Why not? No doubt the parents will pay the necessary entry fee and this will be much cheaper for them than entering him as an external candidate elsewhere. They may even be willing to pay for invigilation, if that proves necessary.

The chances are, given the background, that he will pass easily enough and so the school will not need to be apprehensive about adverse effects on its examination statistics. A 100% pass rate in any subject always looks well!

There are some circumstances when the work outside school time is carried on with the school's blessing, but this brings other problems in its train:

Q. Is it legal to make a charge for instrumental music lessons given by a peripatetic teacher outside normal school hours, if the pupils are going to be entered for the GCSE?

A. It is illegal to make a charge for any tuition or facilities which form part of the school curriculum or are part of the preparation for a public examination for which the school is entering the pupils. What you describe seems to fall within this definition and you should not, therefore, make a charge.

I suspect that it would be possible to prepare pupils for the examination without the instrumental enhancement and this gives you a good case for asking parents to make a voluntary contribution, as opposed to a charge, in order to preserve this valuable addition to the basic provision.

This question introduced the whole issue of the cost of examinations. Entry fees for public examinations is a significant item in the budget for all secondary schools and one which is largely outside the governors' control.

Q. Our allocation for examination fees under the LMS formula falls well short of what we actually spend. Can we fix a limit on the number of GCSE entries we will pay for (e.g. Core and Foundation subjects only), and charge parents for any additional entries?

A. No. The Education Reform Act (Section 106) stipulates that no charge may be made for any entry for a public examination for which a pupil has been prepared in the school. If you wish to save any money on this, the only remedy is not to enter them at all, but I suspect that parents might have something to say about that.

Just by way of an eccentric thought, however, you might just consider whether there is any great point in entering your very brightest pupils for examinations which they do not actually need. If you know they are going into the sixth form and you can assess their performance internally, do they really need the GCSE certification in every subject? I fear, however, that this is an idea for which the time is not right. Your parents will insist upon the examinations and you will need the statistics of good results to ensure your school's place in a meaningless league table. It is interesting to speculate on how much money we might save if things were otherwise, though.

Q. My school wishes to consider switching from traditional A levels to the International Baccalaureate, but we do not think we can afford the higher entry fees which this will involve. Are you aware of any funds upon which we might call for assistance?

A. I am not, although I commend your willingness to consider this very interesting and challenging step. There are some other schools and colleges who have adopted this course and, if you are able to identify and contact them through the IB organization, they may be able to offer advice.

The other possibility is to approach the major employers in your own area. It may well be that one of them, or perhaps the Chamber of Commerce, would be willing to act as a sponsor, in return for local publicity and recognition.

A small saving might be achieved by not entering certain pupils, but there may be parental pressure to overcome:

Q. I am teaching a boy for whom English is his second language and his level of attainment is extremely low. Do we have to enter him for the GCSE in English, when he will not even be able to understand the paper?

A. As things stand at the moment, no, you do not. The governors of your school have the right to determine not to enter him for any specific examination on educational grounds. The question of assessment of the National Curriculum at Key Stage 4 is still under consideration by the new School Curriculum and Assessment Authority, who will have to take a view about the appropriate response to youngsters like this.

There is much to be said for a system of assessment which moves away from age-related testing towards measuring the attainment of pupils at the levels appropriate to the progression of their own learning.

Not all assessment is based on the examination. Coursework plays a significant part in many subjects and can generate problems of its own:

Q. What is the school's obligation in respect of excluded pupils who have been entered for GCSE examinations involving coursework?

A. It is the duty of the Head, whenever exclusions would lead to the loss of the opportunity to take any public examination, to inform the LEA and the governing body without delay of the period of exclusion and the reasons for it. If the LEA or governing body direct that the pupil should be reinstated, the Head must comply with it. Whether the exclusion of a pupil who has a coursework obligation would lead to the loss of the opportunity to enter the examination is a matter for the judgement of the Head in the particular circumstances. Much would depend on the length of the exclusion and the nature of the work to be done.

If the exclusion is upheld by the governing body and by the LEA, if an appeal is made, the school has no further obligation in the matter, although some schools may be prepared to offer the opportunity of submitting the coursework and sitting the examination, without reinstatement.

The conduct of the examinations is an important matter, if the integrity of the system is not to be undermined.

Q. Are there rules about who may invigilate examinations?

A. The rules relating to the conduct of public examinations are laid down by the examining body and it is the responsibility of the Head of the Centre where the examinations are held to ensure that the rules are observed.

Rules vary between the various bodies, each of which publishes its own version. A typical example states that invigilators must be 'suitably qualified and experienced people', but leaves it to the discretion of the Head of Centre to decide who is suitably qualified and experienced. The rules specify, however, that no relative of a candidate and no teacher who has been responsible for the preparation of candidates for the subject being examined shall be the sole invigilator. Examining bodies will normally supply copies of their rules on request and all schools which act as Centres will have them.

The Head of Centre, normally the headteacher, may delegate the administration to someone else, but the ultimate responsibility is not delegated. Making sure the invigilation is properly carried out is part of that responsibility.

Q. We shall be employing invigilators for some of our external examinations this year. Do we have to pay them in the same way as supply teachers?

A. Not necessarily. If you take on supply teachers and then ask them to invigilate, you must pay them as supply teachers. Many schools take the view, however, that invigilation is not teaching and employ non-teachers or teachers, who are happy to accept the job, exclusively for this function. There are no nationally agreed rates for invigilators and schools are, therefore, free to set their own terms. Presumably, market forces operate and schools will wish to ensure that they offer enough to attract competent and responsible people.

Invigilators must be fully briefed on their duties and on the conditions which must be observed. These may vary, depending on the subject or the paper.

Q. Are candidates allowed to use calculators in public examinations?

A. This is a matter for each examining authority to decide. It is quite common nowadays for the use of calculators to be permitted, unless they are specifically prohibited by the syllabus of the particular subject. In some Mathematics papers, where the candidate's own mental calculation skills are being tested, the use of a calculator would obviously be banned.

Because of the sophistication of many modern calculators, the examination authority may well lay down rules governing their use. For example, they would have to be cordless and silent, so as not to disturb other candidates, and any information or programs stored in an electronic memory would have to be cleared beforehand. Candidates would not be able to appeal for special consideration if the calculator failed or if its batteries ran out and borrowing from another candidate once the examination had started would not be allowed. Some schools might decide to make calculators available from stock for the use of candidates, but there is no obligation upon them to do so.

If something goes wrong, the examination authority is likely to take a strong view:

Q. The examination board which our school uses has told us that a particular teacher, who made a mistake with an examination last summer, must not do work in connection with their examinations again. Have they the right to do this and what should be my response as Head?

A. A school which becomes a centre for the examinations of any board enters into a contractual undertaking to act as the agent for the board and to conduct the examinations and all matters related to them in accordance with the rules which the board lays down. Therefore, when the board's rules are broken, as I presume they were in this case, the board determines its response and the centre has little option, if it wishes to continue to be a centre, but to accept it.

The board, however, has no disciplinary powers of its own, other than to decline to do business with a centre or a named individual. Sometimes, when there is a serious infringement of the rules, for example one which involves deliberate dishonesty, a board will expect that the school employing that person will take disciplinary action of its own. Should the school fail to do so, the board could take that omission as a reason for withdrawing recognition of the centre.

Given that the facts of the case are accepted, you have no alternative but to comply with the board's ruling and to keep the teacher concerned well away from all work connected with that board's examinations. If the teacher maintains a good record for several years, you might be in a position to ask the board to reconsider its position. In the meantime, you should also consider whether the misconduct was such as to warrant disciplinary action, such as a warning, on your part.

Having prepared pupils for the examinations, many teachers are involved in moderating coursework and also, in a private capacity, in marking scripts. This latter activity is quite separate from their work as teachers and should be done in their own time. The answer, quoted above, which I gave on the subject of private tuition on school premises, prompted a further query about marking scripts:

Q. You have made it clear that a teacher should not conduct private teaching on school premises. I should be interested to know your view on whether this applies to those who carry out moderating and marking for examination while they are at school.

A.   This is a nice one! My view on teachers taking private classes during school time is quite clear, not least because of the confusion likely to be caused in the minds of parents and pupils about the responsibility for what is being done. No such confusion is likely with the work which you mention.

Technically, though, the same ruling should apply. In practice, however, Heads do not customarily direct teachers on the use to which they put their non-contact time during school hours. They may mark school work, prepare lessons, take a nap, chat with their colleagues or even pop out to visit the bank. Heads rely upon the clause in the *School Teachers' Pay and Conditions of Service Document* which refers to the unspecified time taken to complete various professional duties, rather than insist that they must follow a strict regime. If, therefore, teachers choose to tackle private business, which is non-specific as to time, during non-contact time at school and to complete school duties in their own time, no one is likely to complain.

I suspect that the essential difference between the two cases is that the one is earning money at a specific time and place, while the other is earning money for a task which may be carried out at any time and has no direct third-party involvement.

I did not anticipate the protest which that reply provoked:

Q. I was aghast to read your opinion that teachers could do external marking in school. Surely all examiners and markers are under a duty of confidentiality and explicitly instructed not to do their work in a public place?

A. Yes, of course they are. It was certainly not my intention to suggest the contrary. The point I was making was that many Heads do not, in practice, object to a teacher using non-teaching time in school to perform tasks which are not related to school work, provided that all school work is properly and punctually performed. The duty of an examiner to observe the rules of the examination board is another issue altogether, but it is quite possible to conceive of situations in a school where marking might be done without infringing those rules.

Finally, there are a number of issues which have cropped up concerning the results of the examinations. Much of the trouble has come from the government's decision to publish performance tables and the consequent outcry from schools which feel, for one reason or another, that the published information does not give a fair representation of their achievements.

Q. We have been entering candidates for public examinations of bodies which do not issue their results until after the submission date for official publication. As a result, the performance of the school will look less impressive than it should. What can we do about this?

A. The publication of results is clearly linked to the GCSE and A level results. There is pressure on the government to change this, but until they do, there is little one can do about the nationally published tables. I see no reason, however, why reference should not be made in the tables which you publish to the fact that certain specified results are yet to come.

   You might also wish to refer to them in next year's publication and you are free, of course, to present the full picture in your annual prospectus.

A particularly vexed question is the ownership of coursework, which can be quite important to candidates in subjects like Art. In English, too, a piece of work may be very personal in its nature.

Q. At a case conference on a pupil from this school, a social worker used as evidence a piece of GCSE coursework written by the pupil. It transpired that this had been given to him by the teacher, without the knowledge of the pupil, her parents or the Head. The parents have complained to the governors. What should they do about it?

A. There is no standard answer to the question of ownership of coursework: much depends on the regulations of the examination board concerned. What is clear, however, is that, whether it is the property of the examination board, the school or the pupil herself, it certainly is not the property of the teacher.

The teacher had no right at all to pass this piece of work to a third party, without the permission of its owner, whoever that was, or without reference to the Head, who would have been best placed to deal with the matter.

As this appears to be a case of an error of judgement, rather than serious misconduct, I would not expect the governors to deal with it. Instead, the Chairman should pass it to the Head, with the request that he should take appropriate disciplinary action, in this case probably an oral warning.

Virtually all public examination results are published during the school holidays. They require immediate attention and are likely to entail the provision of a counselling and advice service to students. These duties are undertaken mainly by senior staff.

Q. It is the practice at this school to require the Heads of Sixth Form and Year 11 to come into school during the school holidays in order to deal with business connected with the publication of examination results. Is this a voluntary activity on their part or an obligation?

A. If it is specified in the job description of these posts that dealing with this business is a part of their job, it might be reasonable to suggest that this commitment falls within the scope of paragraph 36(1)(f) of the *School Teachers' Pay and Conditions of Service Document*. This states that there are some tasks which fall outside the 1265 hours of directed time, but which are a necessary part of the job.

As these teachers are probably paid several increments in recognition of their important responsibilities, they might feel that it would be difficult to do their jobs to their own satisfaction, if they did not regard this work as integral to their posts.

The alternative would be to allocate a set time for this work and include it within the directed time of these teachers. I suspect that, for most conscientious teachers at this level, the issue might have the same relevance as the debate about angels dancing on pinheads.

12

School discipline: Exclusions

In a society which has become more and more conscious of human rights and individual freedom, the maintenance of good order in schools has become an issue of public concern, exposing attitudes which are at best ambivalent and frequently contradictory.

On the one hand, a school which enjoys a reputation for high standards of discipline is almost universally seen as 'good' – and a school where pupils are said to be free to do as they please is 'bad' – while, on the other hand, schools experience a degree of confrontation, in dealing with individual cases, which makes the maintenance of high standards both difficult and time-consuming. To the harassed Heads and their staffs, the message appears all too often to be that parents want them to be tough with other people's children.

Since 1986, schools have also faced the task of managing discipline within a legal framework which has been increasingly provided by statute and regulation rather than by the common law, which had previously governed most aspects of teacher–pupil relations. This, in turn, has encouraged both pupils and parents to adopt a legalistic approach, where procedural issues can become more important than the inculcation of good standards of personal behaviour.

The most important aspect of state intrusion into school discipline is the law relating to exclusion from school. In the Education (No. 2) Act 1986, the government put an end to expulsion and suspension in state schools and created the concept of exclusion. Exclusion could be for a fixed term, originally a maximum of five days in any one term, indefinite or permanent. In the Education Act 1993, the indefinite exclusion was controversially abolished and the fixed-term maximum was extended to fifteen days. Apart from prescribing the range of punishment in this area, the legislation also created an apparatus of hearings and appeals, which gave much trouble to schools and a field day for lawyers, both barrack-room and otherwise.

One thing was clear: there was only one way in which a pupil, who was not ill, could be denied access to the school.

Q. If I suggest to parents that they keep their child at home for some days because of his misbehaviour at school, does this count as an exclusion?

A. Yes, it does, you are really making a semantic distinction here, which has no legal basis. The Education (No. 2) Act 1986 defines the removal of a pupil from school as exclusion and lays down the various procedures which must be followed when it is done. As parents have a legal duty to ensure that their children attend school regularly, your proposal that they should not carry out that duty is just another way of saying that you are excluding. You should follow the normal procedures.

The teaching profession regretted the removal of the option of indefinite exclusion in 1993 and Heads in particular have campaigned for its restoration. The case for it was, and is, that time is sometimes needed to persuade parents to face up to their share of responsibility for the behaviour of their offspring.

Q. We have a pupil currently excluded from the school for a relatively minor offence who really ought to be back in school by now. The exclusion is being continued, however, because the parents are refusing to come to see the Head to discuss it. Is this fair on the pupil?

A. Your question might, with equal if not more justice, be put to the parents, who, I assume, have no good reason, such as illness or incapacity, for their obduracy. Although pupils are under the care of the school while they are there, this does not absolve parents from responsibility for their good behaviour. It is entirely reasonable, therefore, for the Head to wish to discuss misconduct which was sufficiently serious to warrant exclusion, however short, before agreeing to reinstatement.

It is none the less true for being a cliché that the school and parents must act in partnership for education to be effective and the school is entitled to expect the full cooperation of parents in insisting upon acceptable standards of behaviour.

I would expect every effort to be made, by letter and by the personal intervention of the Education Welfare Officer, to persuade the parents to comply with the Head's request. In the end, it is the duty of the LEA to ensure that the pupil attends school and, given that attendance is being deliberately prevented by the parents, not the school, there might ultimately be a case for prosecuting the parents for being in breach of the law.

Even with indefinite exclusion, the LEA could intervene and fix a date for reinstatement, a point which was made by a correspondent, who also raised the question of what constituted an excludable offence:

Q. In your comments on indefinite exclusion, you omitted to state that, where a school refuses to fix a date for reinstatement, the LEA has a duty to do so. Was it proper, in any case, to exclude for a minor offence?

A. In a brief answer, I did not cover all aspects of the case, but simply those which were prompted by the question. You are right in referring to the LEA's responsibilities, but it was clear that the school was entirely ready to arrange reinstatement, if only the parents would discuss the issue first. In those circumstances, as I suggested, the LEA should support the school's efforts to secure parental cooperation.

As to the offence itself, the question said it was 'relatively minor', which suggested to me that it was serious enough, in the Head's view, to warrant a short period of exclusion, but well short of permanent exclusion. Given the lack of cooperation from the parents, it may also have been the case that the Head was using exclusion as a means of drawing the parents into a consideration of the pupil's bad behaviour over some time, when less drastic measures had failed to elicit a satisfactory response.

Since the 1993 Act, the best the school could hope for would be to persuade the parents to respond within 15 days. Many Heads explain the significant increase in permanent exclusions as a consequence of the ending of indefinite exclusion.

Even when the parents can be persuaded to appear, the Head's troubles are not necessarily over:

Q. Having excluded a pupil for a serious breach of discipline, I was willing to readmit him, provided that I could obtain reasonable assurances of support from the parents. While they were willing to talk to me, they refused to do so except in front of their son. Am I entitled to insist on seeing them alone?

A. While one can understand why parents might adopt this attitude, in order to appear to be supportive of their son in his eyes, I do not think you are being unreasonable in your view that there are some things better discussed only with the parents. If this is your normal policy in such circumstances, it might not be a bad idea to spell it out in the school prospectus, so that parents know what to expect. The law has nothing to say in the matter and it is probable that your LEA or governors' policy statement is equally silent.

In the situation confronting you, therefore, the best course has to be negotiation, rather than confrontation. You will not wish to be seen to be punishing the child for the obduracy of his parents, any more than you will want to be seen to concede totally to the parents. An opportunity for mediation should be sought here, perhaps using the good offices of the Education Welfare Officer.

Having said that, I have to add that my experience of such cases has been that it is sometimes a very salutary experience for parents and offspring alike to listen together to a full explanation of misbehaviour. It can prove very effective in preventing that all too common problem of the cunning miscreant playing off one side against the other.

The decision to exclude a pupil is not an end but a beginning, as the processes of hearings and appeals are invoked by parents. Only the Head has the power to exclude, but the option of reinstatement is open first to the governing body and second, for LEA schools, to the local authority.

Although the law sets out what the stages in the process should be, it does not lay down how those stages should be conducted:

Q. Is there a model procedure for the conduct of a hearing of an appeal against exclusion?

A. No, but, if principles of natural justice are followed, it is not difficult to establish a simple model which combines an appropriate degree of informality with the opportunity for all concerned to express their point of view. The best approach would be something similar to the following:

- The Chair welcomes all the participants and explains the procedure which is to be followed, ensuring particularly that the parents understand what is to happen.
- The Head, or other member of staff, presents a report on the incident or incidents which led to the exclusion and the reasons why he or she believes that the decision should stand. A written report may be submitted in support of the case. Normally, this will have been circulated in advance and a copy supplied to the parents. All documentary material presented to the panel should be available to the parents.
- The parents (or someone speaking on their behalf), and members of the panel, may question the Head about the presentation.
- The parents (or someone speaking on their behalf) presents their case for reinstatement, calling any evidence in support if they wish to do so.
- The Head or members of the panel may ask questions arising from this presentation.
- The panel withdraws, without the Head, to consider its decision, which may be communicated straight away or subsequently in writing.

There are parents who adopt a legalistic approach to the whole business, behaving as if their child was being brought before a court:

Q. The parents of an excluded pupil are demanding that they should be represented by a barrister at the governors' hearing of the case. Do they have that right?

A. This does seem a bit 'over the top' for a meeting which, as was originally intended, should be a discussion about the best interests of the pupil. Nevertheless, requests for representation at hearings of this kind are becoming more and more common and governors have to decide what their response should be.

While there is no automatic right for parents or pupil to be accompanied by a 'friend', who might, or might not, be a lawyer, it is difficult to argue against the proposition that parents who do not feel confident about their own ability to handle such situations should invite, or hire, someone to assist them. Governors also have to consider that there is the option of an appeal against their decision and they need to take care, therefore, to uphold the principles of natural justice in the way in which they conduct their hearings.

Governors should not allow themselves to be intimidated by the presence of lawyers. Their hearing is not a court of law and they should not allow lawyers to try to turn it into one. They are not bound by the rules of evidence, nor are they required to establish the guilt of the excluded pupil beyond all reasonable doubt. All they are required to do is to decide whether the Head's decision to exclude was, in all the material circumstances, reasonable.

The practice of using lawyers underlines the importance of training for governors, so they do not confront such situations unprepared. They need to be able to resist the pressure of skilled advocates, when it is appropriate to do so, and they should always bear in mind the advice which was given in the DES circular 7/87:

> *'The Secretary of State trusts that LEAs and governing bodies will not use their power to direct reinstatement of excluded pupils hastily and without careful consideration of the consequences for the maintenance of discipline in schools and the position of the headteacher and his staff.'*

The good advice of the Secretary of State has not always been given the consideration it deserves:

Q. Does the LEA have the power to reinstate a permanently excluded pupil when the parents have not lodged an appeal?

A. Yes. The relevant legislation is the Education (No. 2) Act 1986, where, in Section 24, it is provided that it is the duty of the local authority, where they have been informed of a permanent exclusion of a pupil, 'to consider, *after consulting the governing body*, whether he should be reinstated immediately, reinstated by a particular date or not reinstated'. The italics are mine: many local authorities are inclined to overlook this important provision and to take action without reference to the governing body.

The question of the parental appeal is dealt with in two stages. When the permanent exclusion is made, the parents must be informed. They then have the right to make representations to the governing body or to the local authority, but this is not described as an appeal in Section 23 of the Act. Section 26 requires the local authority to make arrangements to enable the parents to appeal against a decision not to reinstate the pupil, that is to say after the local authority has considered the case and made its decision.

Q. The Appeals Panel of our LEA is taking a very aggressive attitude to the exclusion of pupils and has ordered reinstatement in several serious cases. The result has been disruptive in schools and has led to a threat of strike action on the part of teachers. What can we do about this?

A. This type of question is occurring with increasing frequency and is a cause for real concern. Local Education Authorities have a statutory duty to provide education for all pupils resident within their area and this duty does not cease when a pupil is excluded. The law also gives parents the right to choose which school they wish their child to attend and that right does not cease with exclusion either, unless the LEA declines to order reinstatement.

Clearly, appeals will sometimes be upheld because, if none ever were, there would be no point in having the procedure. Where, however, there seems to be a lack of awareness on the part of the Appeals Panel of the consequences of their decisions in certain cases, the only expedient open to schools is to try, through whatever consultation machinery the LEA operates, to impress upon local politicians, who sit on such panels, the seriousness of the situations which they are creating by failing to look beyond the pupil or family in front of them to the broader issues. If this discussion takes place away from the tensions provoked by particular cases, it may be possible to foster a better mutual understanding.

There have been a number of cases where the reinstatement of an excluded pupil has caused such strong feeling that they have been reported in the national press. Most commonly, the teachers in the affected school have threatened not to teach the pupil.

Q. There was considerable press coverage of a strike of teachers in a London school who were refusing to teach a pupil reinstated after exclusion. Was this strike not illegal?

A. The information I have on this incident suggests that it was not illegal, in that the union involved had held a ballot beforehand and followed the usual procedures. The purpose of the strike was, I presume, to demonstrate opposition to the decision taken by the LEA to reinstate a pupil, who had been permanently excluded by the Head as a result of an alleged act of arson. The right to take strike action when an employer does something which employees find intolerable is fundamental to democracy.

Your reference to illegality relates, perhaps, to the refusal to teach the pupil. Here, the teachers were on less safe ground. The right of an LEA to direct the reinstatement of a permanently excluded pupil is firmly based in law. When this happens, it is the duty of the Head to accept the pupil back and to ensure that he or she is properly taught. The Head, therefore, has no option but to direct teachers to teach him or her and a refusal to do so places them in breach of their conditions of service and, potentially, at risk of disciplinary action.

My mailbag indicates that this problem is arising too often for comfort, even if it seldom goes as far as strike action, and it demonstrates the inadequacy of legal answers to difficult human questions.

Clearly, it is right and fair that there should be an appeal procedure against permanent exclusion orders and there would be no point in having an appeal machinery if, once in a while at least, appellants did not win. What is equally clearly wrong, however, is that too many appeals are granted without sufficient regard to the interests of the school and of the pupils and staff who work there. Because LEAs have, as a matter of policy and cost-saving, reduced the amount of separate provision for pupils who are disruptive or who have special needs, they are often faced with no alternative means of fulfilling their statutory duty to provide education but to return the pupil to the same school, especially if the parent insists that this is the school of their choice.

Where different parts of the law are at odds with each other, as they are here, the remedy can only be in further legal provision. What is lacking at the moment is a sanction which would limit the normal freedom of choice of the parent of the pupil who has committed serious disciplinary offences. In short, the strike which provoked your question arose from a situation where rights and duties are out of balance.

Even if the LEA decides to send the pupil to another school, there may still be problems. There are many instances of schools working together by sharing the most intractable disciplinary cases between them, but, where such cooperation does not exist, there may well be trouble:

Q. Do Heads and governors have no rights at all when LEAs insist on reinstating disruptive pupils? Could they not, for instance, insist that the parents sign a contract of good behaviour?

A. At the time of writing, the only right which governors have is to appeal against the LEA ruling. Unfortunately, appeals panels do not have a good record of siding with governors. The most a school can do is to argue their case up to the point where the LEA issues a written direction to admit the pupil and then to give in under protest.

There are indications that the government has become more sympathetic to schools in this matter and there is a possibility that legislation will be introduced to strengthen the schools' position. Measures under consideration include the removal of the parental right to choose a school, after a pupil has been twice excluded permanently, strengthening the guidance to Appeals Panels, obliging them to take into account the interests of the majority of the pupils in the school, and an increase in the provision of Pupil Referral Units.

Pupil Referral Units (PRUs) could be particularly useful, especially if it is a requirement that permanently excluded pupils must attend one prior to any possibility of a return to mainstream education.

The contract idea is less easy to legislate for. Many schools already use agreements between school and parents, either as a standard admissions procedure or to deal with cases of indiscipline. They are useful, in that they do confront parents with their share of responsibility in the partnership which should exist, but they are of no real help with parents who do not want to cooperate, or who do not know how to.

To call these agreements contracts is a misuse of the term, because they are not legally binding agreements and there is no machinery to enforce them. No government is likely to introduce a law which would, in effect, deprive some young people of the right to be educated. They may well decide, however, that the power of schools to secure good standards of behaviour is in need of enhancement.

The parents of excluded pupils often react emotionally to problems with which they are unable to cope:

Q. Following the exclusion of a boy, his father came into the school and threatened three members of staff with violence. What is the Head's appropriate response?

A. Uttering threats of violence is, of course, potentially an offence which could be reported to the police, but, unless the incident was very serious or one in a series, a Head might not wish to go that far in dealing with it.

One presumes that the father's behaviour was occasioned by his anger and shock at his son's exclusion and he needs the assurances that this was based on a fair investigation of what the boy had done and that the proper procedures will be followed, in which he will have an ample opportunity to express his views. Although these procedures may be well understood by teachers, many parents are not aware of them at all until they are faced with personal involvement.

At the same time, his behaviour was entirely unacceptable and the staff will want to know that the Head is taking appropriate steps to prevent it happening again. If this was an isolated case, it may be sufficient to write to the parent to advise him that he must not come into the school without making an appointment with the Head, or another senior member of staff, and that, if he were to threaten staff again, the matter would certainly be reported.

In serious cases, the advice can be made mandatory by the LEA or, in grant-maintained schools, by the governing body, with the consequence that, if he were to come onto school premises without an appointment, he could be removed by the police.

Being unable to cope with the situation takes many forms:

Q. This school has been confronted by parents who bring their son into school every day, in spite of the fact that he has been excluded. They say that they are both at work and cannot take care of him. What can we do?

A. An exclusion, which has been carried out through the proper processes, has the force of law behind it, which means, if one took matters to a logical conclusion, that a court order could be obtained to restrain the parents from this entirely unreasonable behaviour.

Short of such an extreme measure, the best the school could do would be to arrange for an Education Welfare Officer to return the lad promptly to the custody of one of his parents, wherever he or she might be. Having him delivered to the workplace might be sufficiently embarrassing to encourage them to seek alternative solutions to their problem.

One should always remember that exclusions affect only a small minority of pupils, but they take up a disproportionate share of time, some of which might be better spent on the majority of pupils.

The situations described here make it clear that there is still much to be done to establish a disciplinary regime which meets the educational needs of pupils, sustains the authority of schools, satisfies parents, pleases politicians and is seen to be fair by everyone. Meanwhile, schools are generally havens of good order and civilized behaviour in a disordered world.

Game'. Although it was a light-hearted comment, it nonetheless illustrates the complex

13

School discipline: In loco parentis

It is part of the folklore of schools, reinforced by the interpretation of common law in the courts, that, when children are in school, teachers take over the role of parent in caring for and controlling them. This common law duty has been increasingly circumscribed by statute and by the closer exploration of the limits of teachers' authority by litigious parents.

The most obvious statutory limitation came in 1986 with the prohibition of corporal punishment, although that still left the sometimes blurred distinction between necessary physical restraint and punishment as an area of contention.

Q. My Head is investigating a complaint from a parent that I assaulted his son, following an incident when I intervened physically to stop the boy bullying another pupil. Have I no rights in this matter?

A. Of course you have, but so have the boy and his father. They have the right to have the incident investigated and you have the right to put forward your account of it.

Since corporal punishment was made illegal in state schools in 1986, physical action by a teacher on a pupil has been limited to the exercise of reasonable restraint to prevent a pupil or pupils doing damage to themselves, other individuals or property. The definition of reasonableness in this context is the amount of physical force required to achieve the objective and no more.

In a case such as the one you describe, if your intervention was limited to pulling the bully away from his victim sufficiently to put an end to his hurting him, that was reasonable. If you then struck him, shook him or pushed him hard against the wall, you might be said to have gone one step too far. No doubt what happened in the heat of the moment was not quite so clear-cut and it may well be that the frustrated bully is more than capable of exaggerating what happened.

Your Head, faced with the complaint, has really no alternative, for your sake as well as the parent's, but to investigate what happened and you must hope that the accounts gathered from others, who may have witnessed the event, together with your own report on it, will resolve the matter. It will have been particularly helpful if you reported the incident immediately after it took place.

As a sensible precaution, you should consult your union or professional association, if you belong to one. It is this kind of incident that makes union membership important for teachers. Should the parent seek to take legal action, for example by complaining to the police – unlikely, I suspect, in this instance – the union would look after your interests.

In the nature of things, pupils are likely to bc involved as witnesses to incidents of this sort and this provoked an interesting question:

Q. If a teacher is subject to a disciplinary hearing for assault against a pupil, do the pupil concerned and others who witnessed the event have to appear at the hearing?

A. This is the sort of situation which one would like to avoid, if at all possible, but the answer in the end may have to be that they do.

Cases of this sort are usually founded on investigations conducted by the Head or another senior person and will include written evidence supplied by pupils who were victims or witnesses. The hope is that these written statements will be accepted by all concerned and make it unnecessary for pupils to face the daunting experience of appearing in person.

However, it is a fundamental principle of natural justice that an accused person has the right to test the strength of the evidence against him and, if need be, to challenge its reliability. From the pupils' point of view, this might best be done by a representative of the defendant interviewing the pupils in the presence of their parents before the hearing takes place. In the last resort, however, the defendant has the right to have the evidence heard and examined in front of the panel.

The other problem which may arise from a complaint of assault occurs when a complaint is made to the police. Whether the complaint is made against a teacher or against a pupil, the police have no alternative but to investigate it.

Q. If the police are investigating a case of assault by a pupil committed at school, should the school cease its own enquiries into the matter?

A. This is always going to be a tricky question, because two different ends are being served. An assault is, of course, an offence and, if it is reported to the police, they have a duty to investigate it and they may well feel that teachers interrogating those concerned before they do may prejudice or distort the outcome. Equally, the record of any investigation which the school does conduct may be handed over to the police as evidence.

On the other hand, the school has every right to investigate and to deal with an obvious breach of discipline on its premises, regardless of whether the police decide to proceed with the case or not and even regardless of any decision which a court may come to. A school is not bound by the rules of evidence which apply in court, although an acquittal would be useful support for an appeal against subsequent disciplinary action.

The answer lies in cooperation. If a pupil is alleged to have committed an offence in school which is serious enough to attract the attention of the police, it would probably justify exclusion while the matter is under investigation. Once it is clear whether the police wish to bring a charge or not, the school can then take its own disciplinary action, which will lose none of its validity by being postponed.

Corporal punishment apart, the power of schools to administer reasonable punishment to pupils while they are in their care is not otherwise disputed, although the justice of doing so in specific cases often is. But, where does the school's authority begin and end?

Q. As Head, I am the subject of strong parental complaints to the governors and to the LEA because I have punished two boys for misconduct outside school hours in the shopping centre close to the school. They say that I have no right to deal with the matter. Are they right?

A. In the last resort, only a court of law could determine whether or not you were right in this, but such precedents as there are tend to support you.

Much would depend upon the circumstances, but if the pupils were on their way, however circuitously, to or from school, or if, by reason of their dress or other evidence, they were easily identified as being pupils at the school, or if their conduct was such as to damage the good reputation of the school, the balance of probability is that your authority to deal with the matter would be upheld.

Your position would be further strengthened if you have, in the school prospectus or school rules, references to the kind of behaviour expected outside the school, which might include, for example, respect for neighbouring property or responsible conduct in the shopping centre.

As in so many matters, the test of reasonableness should be applied to this. The local community expects a school to insist on decent standards of behaviour and does not always want that to stop at the school gate. At the same time, misconduct committed completely outside the context of the school is the responsibility of parents and teachers should be hesitant to intervene.

A great deal turns on the circumstances and the next example was more clear-cut:

Q. Is abusing a teacher in the street an offence for which exclusion is an appropriate sanction?

A. There are two questions here and the answer to both is yes.

On the rare occasions when the issue has been challenged in the courts, it has been held that a school is within its rights in imposing sanctions upon a pupil who acts in a way which undermines the discipline and authority of the school. Given that the abuse is being perpetrated by a pupil upon a teacher because he or she is a teacher, the school is fully justified in taking steps to deal with it.

Whether exclusion is an appropriate sanction depends on the gravity of the offence and the record of the offender, but it may be employed, as may any other sanction normally used by the school.

Some cases, however, turn out to be of the sort that keep our learned friends so gainfully employed:

Q. We are faced with the problem of a truant who behaved badly off the school premises. He was found smoking in a public place and was defiant when confronted there by a member of staff. He was excluded, but told he could return if he apologized for his rudeness. He refuses to do so and his parents demand readmission on the grounds that he committed no offence against the school. What should we do?

A. In my view, this boy has committed two offences, both of which justify punishment: truancy and rudeness. Your disciplinary action appears to have concentrated on the latter and is not, on the face of it, unreasonable.

There have been very few cases where the right of a school to discipline its pupils for off-site offences has been called into question and such precedents as there are indicate a willingness on the part of judges to support the authority of the school.

It could be argued that the teacher who confronted the boy with smoking had picked the wrong issue, particularly if he was not wearing school uniform and could not have been associated with the school at the time. His behaviour was the responsibility of his parents, not the school. The teacher would have been well within his rights, if he had challenged him on his truancy.

Whether the teacher was right or wrong, however, the rudeness was unacceptable. If a pupil behaves in an offensive manner towards someone he knows to be a teacher at his school, he is deliberately showing a disrespect for the school's authority. Moreover, assuming that the event took place when he should have been at school, he committed the offence at a time when he should have been under the school's authority and when, presumably, his parents believed that he was.

Only a court could decide whether my interpretation is correct in the light of all the facts, but I believe that you have ample justification for standing your ground, especially if you enjoy the support of your governors in continuing the exclusion.

Naturally, when children do misbehave off the school premises, the public is quick to point the finger at the school, especially when the misbehaviour occurs in the local shops:

Q. Is it acceptable for the school to ban pupils from entering a shop near the school? We have had numerous reports of bad behaviour there, which damages the school's reputation.

A. Certainly. Unless you have released pupils into the care of their parents at lunch-time, you are responsible for the supervision of their conduct. On those grounds alone, you are fully entitled to determine where they should and should not go.

Equally, you are responsible for maintaining the good name of your school and you are therefore right to impose sanctions on the misconduct of pupils, who may be identified as such, even though the incidents take place outside the school premises.

Of course, the key issue there was whether the pupils were in the care of the school at the material time or not. Assuming the misconduct took place during the lunch-break, were they pupils who remained in the care of the school, but were allowed to leave the premises, or were they pupils who went home (or elsewhere) at lunch-time, at the parents' behest? In practice, the school's right to crack the whip is unlikely to be challenged.

The question of who is in charge of pupils is always a problem when it comes to school buses:

Q. As Deputy Head, I am fed up of dealing with constant complaints from a bus driver about the behaviour of our pupils on the way to and from school. Does he not have some responsibility for controlling them?

A. Certainly he does, or rather the proprietor of the company with whom your school or local authority has the contract for the service.

Properly speaking, the pupils do not come under the school's control until they enter the school premises and, while they are travelling to and from school, whether by bus or otherwise, they remain the responsibility of their parents. There is no essential difference here between travelling by a regular public transport service and by a hired vehicle contracted for the purpose: the responsibility for the conduct of passengers rests with the provider of the service.

Not all bus drivers are adept at persuading young people to behave properly and, access to parents being rather difficult, inevitably they turn to the school for help when things go wrong. Inevitably, too, because schools wish to promote good behaviour and maintain a reputation for so doing, Heads and Deputies spend an inordinate amount of time dealing with their complaints and, because the school's reputation is in question, the school has the right to punish pupils for such misconduct.

Nevertheless, the responsibility does rest with the contractor and, if there are problems, a non-driving assistant should be provided by him to ensure good conduct and, in particular, that the driver is not distracted.

The question of the teacher's responsibilities outside the school premises has been covered in Chapter 1. What about inside? Are pupils automatically the responsibility of the school as soon as they pass through the gates?

Q. Many of our pupils arrive on the school site before any of the staff. What responsibility do I, as Head, have for their supervision? Should I bring staff in? Should I close the gates?

A. This is one of those areas in which you can be expected to do only what is reasonable in the circumstances. It is in the nature of things that some pupils are going to arrive early and the sensible policy is to allow them onto the site, having taken care to see that there are no obvious hazards to their safety. It is also sensible to arrange a rota of staff on duty before school starts in order to supervise an orderly entry and start to the day. In most schools, ten minutes is seen as reasonable for this, although, if there are special circumstances, such as early buses, a longer period may be necessary.

It is important that these arrangements are communicated to parents, for example in the school prospectus, so that they know the time when supervision begins and are aware that, if they send their children to school earlier, they will not be supervised. If you have special arrangements for allowing pupils to enter the buildings in inclement weather, these, too, should be explained.

If the parents have sent them, must the school supervise them outside the normal session times?

Q. We have a boy who is entitled to free school meals but whose behaviour during the lunch-break is quite intolerable. Does his entitlement to a meal mean that we cannot exclude him from the premises at lunch-time?

A. There is no legal obligation on a school to keep pupils on site between sessions, although where, as is commonly the case, pupils are allowed to remain, there is a legal duty to ensure that they are properly supervised.

Where a pupil's conduct is unacceptable, it is a legitimate sanction to exclude him or her from the premises during that period, having informed the parents that they must assume responsibility for him or her until school restarts.

The fact of entitlement to a free meal does not prevent the imposition of this sanction. The entitlement is to a meal. It is not an entitlement to a specific type of meal, nor to a place in which to eat it, nor to supervision while it is being eaten. The requirement can be met by preparing a packed meal for this pupil, to be collected before leaving the premises.

The question may also be posed the other way round:

Q. Is it safe or sensible to allow pupils to leave school premises other than at the end of sessions?

A. Like so much else concerning the responsibilities of schools, it all depends upon the circumstances.

It is in order to allow pupils to leave at the request of parents, where there is good reason shown for doing so. Medical appointments or other special events of which written notice has been given are obvious examples.

Equally, where pupils leave the premises, accompanied by a teacher, for example to work on a project which takes them out into the community, this is acceptable, although one would expect that parents would be informed in advance of the arrangements for such an activity.

When pupils are suspended or taken ill, it is not advisable to allow them to leave the premises ahead of the normal time, except in the care of a parent, or other responsible adult.

It is not uncommon for older pupils to be sent on errands from the school, for example to purchase goods from a shop or to deliver a message. Great care is needed here and it is desirable that a school should have established guidance to staff about it. While a pupil is in school, the teachers act *in loco parentis* and it is expected, therefore, that a teacher should exercise the same care and control as a reasonable parent.

So, if a pupil is deemed old enough and responsible enough to be entrusted with the errand, if it is felt that he or she (preferably they – it is probably unwise to send one alone) will not be exposed to undue risk or danger and if clear instructions are given, then it may not be unreasonable to allow it. But the question must always be asked: if something dreadful happens, can the school defend its decision?

Teachers spend a great deal of time trying to discover culprits of misconduct and ensuring that justice is done. Happily, they are not constrained in their investigation by 'judges' rules' of evidence, nor do they have to prove a case beyond reasonable doubt. Provided that they are satisfied that they have established the truth, that is sufficient. Care needs to be taken with investigation, however. Not everything may be acceptable.

Q. Does a teacher have the right to search a pupil's possessions?

A. Pupils have just as much right to privacy as anyone else and their personal possessions are entitled to respect. Teachers are, however, *in loco parentis* when pupils are in their care and may, with good reason, act as a responsible parent might in checking lockers or personal possessions.

Care should be exercised in searching personal bags or clothing. The best approach is to invite the pupil to turn out the bag or pockets voluntarily. A forced search would be ill-advised and where a pupil refuses, it would be wise to invite a parent to attend so that a search may be made.

It is also a requirement that punishment should be reasonable and appropriate to the offence and the offender. The test of reasonableness may not be straightforward. The gymnasium is often a testing ground:

Q. If pupils come to PE lessons without the appropriate clothing, are the PE staff entitled to enforce participation by loaning clothing from stock or by wearing (or not wearing) other clothing?

A. 'Please, Sir, I haven't got my kit', was always the last resort of the desperate as well as the genuinely forgetful and PE teachers have always been vigorous and often inventive in devising ways of discouraging such exasperating conduct.

Difficulties tend to arise when a teacher introduces a new method of retaliation without notice or one which upsets parents or pupils. The important point is that whatever system is used, it should be accepted as school policy, be published to parents and pupils and be enforced evenhandedly by all teachers concerned.

Q. It is a school rule that all pupils should take a shower after PE lessons. What can we do with a boy who refuses to do so?

A. It is difficult to give a general answer to what must be a very specific question relating to this one pupil. The reason for his refusal must be established before deciding what to do and it will probably be advisable to bring the parents into the discussion.

It is not in the school's interests that one boy should be able to disobey a sensible rule indefinitely, nor is it in the boy's interests that he should be allowed to neglect basic personal hygiene. Adolescents are often very sensitive about their bodies and the existence of communal showers may lie at the root of the problem. Whatever it is, a patient and sympathetic approach is more likely to succeed than an authoritarian insistence on immediate compliance.

14

School discipline: Dress, drugs and detention

It is, perhaps, not entirely surprising that the issues of discipline that most concern Heads and their staffs do not arise from the normal routines of classroom life. Most of the problems of discipline are more general in character and one topic which comes up very regularly is the way in which pupils present themselves at school.

This is mainly a problem for secondary schools but, with school uniform increasingly becoming a feature in primary schools too, they may also be affected.

Since 1986, governing bodies have had the power to establish standards for the dress and personal appearance of pupils. They may decide to have a uniform, or not to do so. They may establish a less formal dress code and they may address such issues as hair length and style and various aspects of personal adornment. The Head translates the governors' wishes into school rules and these are subject both to the test of reasonableness and to any legislation which may impinge upon them, which is another way of saying that things are never as simple as they look.

For instance:

Q. Our school rule that girls are not allowed to wear trousers has been challenged by a parent. The governors are unwilling to give way, but are they vulnerable in law?

A. Yes, they are. It is obvious that your school is not located in an area where there are Moslem pupils. If it were, I suspect that you would have been faced with this question long ago, put by parents whose faith decrees that a woman's legs should be covered. In any case, it is highly likely that, were your governors to be challenged under the Equal Opportunities legislation, they would lose.

Of course, they may stick to their guns so long as they are not threatened with court action, but I doubt whether they would get any support from an LEA to fight off a legal challenge on the issue. Incidentally, have your governors ever asked themselves what their attitude would be to a Scottish boy appearing in school in his kilt?

Most adolescents simply cannot resist the temptation to supplement the handiwork of nature with all manner of embellishments, most of which have little appeal to the adult eye.

Q. My governors are insisting that there should be a school rule preventing boys from wearing jewellery, although they seem to be prepared to take a more tolerant view for girls. What is my position, as Head?

A. Governing bodies in maintained schools have the right, if they choose to exercise it, of drawing up statements of general principles for the discipline of their schools. They are not obliged to do so but, when they do, Heads should not disregard them. They may need to be reminded, however, that the internal management and control of the school is the responsibility of the Head, under the *School Teachers' Pay and Conditions of Service Document*.

A statement of principles might well refer to the general standard of behaviour expected of pupils to their personal appearance and to school dress. The detailed rules and their promulgation and enforcement are the responsibility of the Head, although the rules should be reported to the governors, so that they can satisfy themselves that their principles are being upheld.

Thus, in the particular case which you cite, it would not be unreasonable of the governors to make a general statement about the wearing of jewellery, but it would be the duty of the Head to warn them that a statement which appeared to discriminate between the sexes might leave them open to challenge under the Equal Opportunities legislation. It is also then the Head's duty to translate that statement into school rules, which are likely to be acceptable to parents and pupils as well as enforceable without too much difficulty.

In practical terms, this requires common sense as well as a regard for the pitfalls of the Equal Opportunities Act. For example, as it is an accepted social custom for many girls to have their ears pierced and to wear 'sleepers' to keep the holes open, it might be thought unreasonable to ban such earrings altogether. If such studs are to be permitted, then it could be discriminatory not to allow boys the same freedom. In these circumstances, a limit of one per ear may achieve the objective of inhibiting over-adornment in both sexes. Similar arguments apply to other items of jewellery, such as rings and pendants.

One last consideration which you have not mentioned is that of safety. In making rules about dress, jewellery and hairstyles, it is always necessary to bear in mind the possible hazards of laboratories and workshops. Here again, the same rules should apply to both sexes.

Some schools manage to get themselves into quite a frenzy about the minutiae of prescribed garments and colours.

Q. A GM school in our area has extended its list of prescribed school clothing to include 'navy outdoor coat/jacket'. Is it reasonable to insist that parents purchase such an item for a growing child and can the school enforce this even to the point of exclusion?

A. A school's policy on dress is the responsibility of the governing body, on which parents are represented. Most schools would also consult parents, through a PTA for instance, before introducing a potentially expensive change. If you object to the policy, you ought first to discover how far there was effective consultation.

At a time when schools have been forced to compete for pupils, there is an assumption, rightly or wrongly, that one of the factors which determines the 'image' of a school is the appearance of its pupils. No doubt this is what has motivated the school in question to try to stop their pupils wearing the highly coloured outer garments which are so popular at the moment.

Whether it is reasonable or not is a matter of opinion. At least the school has confined itself to specifying only the colour, leaving a choice which could range from a plastic mack to an overcoat. I suspect that they may be making some trouble for themselves over the definition of 'navy' and over cuffs, collars and patches of contrasting colours.

As for enforcement, the law does give the governing body the power to set standards of school dress and thus, by inference, the power to exclude from the school those who refuse unreasonably to conform. Were the matter to be brought to a court, the issue would probably turn on whether the rule was a reasonable one within the law and whether the refusal to conform could reasonably be justified. I do not know what the answer would be in this case and finding out might prove more expensive than a navy-blue anorak.

And then there's hair. With boys, though never with girls, it is the length. With girls, and sometimes with boys, it is the style or the colour.

Q. Is it reasonable to exclude a girl who has come to school with her hair dyed in purple and green stripes or a boy who has his hair halfway down his back?

A. If you have a school rule or a school code on pupil appearance which says that hair should be only in a natural colour and not exceeding a certain length, and if this rule is known to pupils and to parents, you are well within your rights in excluding them until they present themselves in an acceptable manner. If you have no such code, but you believe that their appearance is detrimental to the good image of the school, you still have the right to insist that they change their styles but, in this case, perhaps you should give them a warning to return better presented on the following day.

If you wish to draw up a code relating to hairstyle, remember that, if your school is mixed, you need to frame appropriate guidance for both sexes in ways which cannot be challenged as discriminatory. It is useful to add, in any case, that, for obvious safety reasons, long hair must always be tied back for PE and Games activities and when working in laboratories and workshops.

The actual length of hair is always a problem, because fashions do change and it is not unreasonable for young people to want to follow. There have been cases of boys excluded for shaving all their hair off, as well as for growing it inordinately long, both gestures being interpreted, probably rightly, as challenges to convention, parents or school authority, according to taste. On the whole, it may be better to stick to concepts of tidiness, cleanliness and conventionality of appearance, rather than to be too precise about length, and so leave yourself greater scope to deal with whatever barrack-room lawyer challenge to authority the more ingenious may devise.

Of course, hair doesn't only grow on heads:

Q. Is a school within its rights in excluding a student for wearing a beard?

A. Yes. If the school rules stipulate that students must be clean-shaven, the school is entitled to enforce it, if necessary by excluding a student who refuses to conform. It might be worth bearing in mind that there are some ethnic minority groups who are naturally hirsute and who generally have strong views about permitting moustaches and beards. Schools might be better advised to stipulate cleanliness and neatness of appearance, rather than getting into problems of defining 'five o'clock shadows'.

Challenges to authority are often very carefully judged:

Q. Can a school prevent a student from sitting an examination because he turns up to school inappropriately dressed?

A. Technically, the answer to this must be 'Yes'. Attendance at school for an examination is in no way different from attendance on any other day and, if a school has a strictly enforced dress code, it is not obliged to relax it. Given that pupils are well aware of the policy, there is equally no reason why the school should not seek to recover the fee from the parents because the pupil has failed without good reason to take the examination.

One has to ask, however, whether an instant response of that nature is the wisest or most humane one. A few pupils every year try this particular ploy, perhaps as a gesture just to 'cock a snook' at authority or maybe even seeking attention at what is, for many, a very stressful time. I knew one pupil who tried this because he did not want to take the exam and thought that this would get him out of it!

I am inclined to think that the best response is to let them get away with it once, but send a prompt message to the parents to insist that there shall be no repetition. One might even, if one has the resources, make them sit the paper in isolation from their peers.

Finally, there is the question of changing from one regime to another:

Q. We wish to change our school uniform. What are the legal constraints on our doing so?

A. The law is largely silent on this matter, other than providing that this, along with other matters relating to the general conduct of the school, is the responsibility of the governing body.

In coming to a decision, therefore, the governors should be guided by considerations of common sense, rather than law. They should be very sensitive to the opinion of parents, and not just the views of a vocal minority. School uniform, especially if it is in any way non-standard in design or colour, can be expensive. Any change should be introduced gradually to allow existing items to wear out or be outgrown. Wide consultation with parents, staff and indeed the pupils themselves will almost certainly enhance the eventual result and ensure that the change is acceptable to the great majority.

The issue of drugs is far more serious and it is one which every secondary school and, many would say, every primary school must address. In a society where drugs are easily obtainable everywhere, schools have been faced with two challenges. The first is to educate children about drugs and, in particular, to ensure that they can have no doubts about the effects which drugs can have on their minds and bodies. The second is to keep the scourge of drug trading and use outside the school.

The educational challenge is now being tackled, with the development of increasingly sophisticated programmes on the subject, adapted for use with the various age groups, starting in the primary school. No school, however well ordered, can afford to neglect this vital subject and, given the amount of material now available, there can be no excuse for doing so.

On the disciplinary side, the issue is more complex. While, on the one hand, schools will wish to support and help children in difficulties and not to make too much of what may, in some cases, be isolated incidents of experimentation, they have to take into account that they are dealing with something which is illegal.

Q. Having found two pupils in the school with cannabis, I have excluded them permanently. Should I inform the police?

A. Yes. It is wrong deliberately to conceal a criminal offence, although I can fully understand that you do not want the school to receive adverse publicity as a result.

The best way to deal with it is to talk to your local beat officer, if you have one, in the hope that he will be able to give you advice on the best course of action. It may well be that the police will not want to charge your two pupils, but they may be very interested in the source of their supply. On the other hand, these pupils deserve the kind of shock that a severe warning from the police would give them and their parents certainly need to be involved in that too.

Not surprisingly, when this response was published, it provoked a sharp response, and this gave me the opportunity to expand on my advice and to make it clear that I believed that schools need to adopt a flexible approach when dealing with offenders.

Q. We found your answer on drugs in schools disturbing. You said nothing about helping the young people involved or about schools seeking professional advice. Surely, permanent exclusion for possessing cannabis is too severe?

A. The response I gave was to a questioner who had already excluded the offenders permanently. He merely asked whether he should inform the police, not whether he had done the right thing.

I believe that schools must take the drugs issue very seriously and, within the constraints of this column, I can only give the briefest indication of the three aspects which I believe should be addressed.

The first must be preventive. Schools should ensure that there is an appropriate programme of education in place at all levels, based upon the best available professional advice, the aim of which is to convince every young person that drugs are for sick people and should only be taken on medical advice.

The second is discipline. I am inclined to agree that permanent exclusion may be too severe for possessing cannabis, although circumstances may alter cases, but I would support temporary exclusion, on the grounds that it ensures that parents are alerted to the situation and brings home to the pupil that the offence is taken extremely seriously. For trading in any form, I would not hesitate to recommend permanent exclusion. Schools have a duty to the great majority of pupils and to their parents not to expose them to unnecessary risks and influences and, in this matter, the policy needs to be crystal clear.

The third is caring for the individual. It is important to try to ensure that any individual pupil who has become involved with drugs should receive the personal support and counselling needed to divert him or her from further dangerous experimentation. It is unlikely that the school will have the resources to provide this service and professional advice should be sought.

Finally, to revert to the issue which provoked the correspondence, I stand by my view that the police should be informed. I know that they are unlikely to be interested in minor instances of possession, which the school itself should deal with, but they should be very interested in tracking down the sources of supply and those, in or out of school, who are doing the trading.

There is one last point, which was not covered in the correspondence, and that is the need to educate teachers. Many teachers, unless they are specifically trained, have little knowledge of drugs and, especially, are not attuned to recognizing the symptoms of drug abuse in their pupils. A fully developed school drugs policy must include the raising of the awareness of the teaching staff to the manifestations of drug use and agreed procedures for investigating suspected cases. The first duty is to protect, the second to educate, and punishment comes in only where the first two have failed.

The question of punishment, as we have seen with exclusions, is far from straightforward, and the question of detention is another contentious issue.

On the general issue of punishment, the law, when its intervention has been invoked, has generally supported the teacher:

Q. Recently, a pupil, who had behaved very badly in the classroom over a considerable period, was punished by being placed in isolation from his peers for a whole school day. His parents are complaining to everyone they can think of, saying that the school has no right to do this and that it is humiliating and inhumane. Do they have any case?

A. Without being in possession of all the facts, one can never be entirely sure but, on the face of it, the parents of this pupil would make better use of their time and energy discussing with the school how they can help them to ensure that their child is less disruptive.

The school has the right, upheld in the past by the courts, to enforce reasonable standards of discipline by the use of punishment, such punishment being reasonable and in proportion to the gravity of the misconduct. The tests of reasonableness and proportionality which a court would use, if the school were to be challenged in law, would be based on what was generally accepted custom and practice in schools and on what a reasonable parent might do in punishing their own child. The court would have regard also to the age of the child and to any other material circumstances.

The court would be most unlikely to accept that any individual parent had the right to dictate what the school could or could not do in this respect. Whether it was a humiliating or inhumane punishment would depend on the actual circumstances, but, given that many parents would consider sending their child to his or her room, deprived of the company of others, a thoroughly normal response to unacceptable behaviour, I find it hard to believe that the parents in this case would succeed.

When it comes to keeping the pupil behind after school, however, the law is much less helpful:

Q. A parent has refused to agree to our keeping her son in detention in the afternoon after school. Do we have the right to do it, whatever she says?

A. I think you would be unwise to do so. Although the courts have supported the right of schools to use detention as a disciplinary sanction, the inference to be drawn from their decisions is that this presupposes that parents have consented to it. To detain someone against their will, except as a consequence of judicial process, is unlawful imprisonment and, in the case of minors, that consent is exercised by their parents.

In DFE Circular 8/94, the issue was addressed somewhat obliquely:

> *'Where any detention imposed is a reasonable response to a disciplinary incident (and where the parents have not expressly withdrawn their permission), the courts have upheld teachers' right to use detention as a punishment.'*

The implication of this is clear enough.

In practice, schools follow a long-accepted code of practice in ensuring that parents are notified in advance of a detention and are invited to sign a return slip indicating that they are aware of, and thus, presumably, consent to the detention taking place. Where parents raise difficulties over transport or appointments, schools are usually willing to agree to the punishment being moved to another time, all of which is sensible, because the school is punishing the pupil, not the parents.

Most schools set out their disciplinary policy in their prospectus, so that detention, if it is given, will not come as a surprise to parents. If they do object, however, it has to be made clear to them that there is a limited range of sanctions available to schools and that, if this one is not acceptable to them, exclusion may be the only alternative available.

This state of affairs is clearly unsatisfactory from the schools' point of view and it must be hoped that government will be persuaded to take a fresh look at the range of sanctions open to schools, with a view to reinforcing the right of teachers, subject to appropriate safeguards, to maintain reasonable standards of discipline.

15
School journeys

It is one of the most admirable aspects of British education that so many teachers are prepared, often in their own time and for no personal gain, to enrich the educational experiences of their pupils by taking them on visits and residential trips, in their own country and abroad.

Every year, thousands of youngsters leave their classrooms and expand their horizons with a wide range of activities, ranging from visits to local museums and field centres to adventure expeditions and journeys overseas.

Inevitably, with so many activities taking place, there are mistakes, accidents and sometimes tragedies, all of which remind us of the great responsibilities which teachers take on when they take their pupils outside their schools. Naturally, especially when accidents happen, parents and the public at large want to be assured that every possible precaution is taken and politicians respond with regulations which, they hope, will make all such activities as safe as possible.

No matter how many regulations are made, the responsibilities and the risks will always remain and we must be grateful to teachers who are willing to take on the burden of looking after other people's children, sometimes in strange and unfamiliar environments. Not surprisingly, Heads and teachers are always anxious to be sure of their rights and duties when they do so.

The first question is, 'Do I have to take every pupil who wants to go?'

Q. The leader of a school party going abroad has declined to take one girl on the grounds that, because of a medical condition, her behaviour is unpredictable. The parents are seeking to appeal to the governors, on the grounds that we are discriminating unfairly against their daughter and depriving her of educational opportunities available to other pupils. What happens if the governors agree with them?

A. Although the governors may, in the interests of maintaining good relations with parents, hear what these parents have to say and although, having heard it, they may seek to persuade the party leader to reconsider his or her decision, they are in no position to require the leader to take the pupil nor to instruct the Head to direct such action.

Whether or not this trip takes place in term or holiday time, it is not a compulsory part of the school curriculum and the teachers responsible for it are undertaking a voluntary activity, which they could not be directed to do. In taking a party of pupils, they are accepting responsibility for them *in loco parentis* and they must be satisfied, therefore, that they can cope with that responsibility in all conceivable circumstances. Faced with a pupil whose record, for whatever reason, gives them cause for doubt about their ability to cope, they are right to decline the responsibility.

It is worth adding that the situation is not changed by the parents signing any form of indemnity, because the duties of a party leader cannot be signed away.

One would like to be more positive, however, in cases of physical or mental handicap, as opposed to indiscipline. Perhaps, if appropriate additional supervision were provided for this girl, which covered the risks which otherwise existed, the party leader might be prepared to accept her on the trip after all.

Bad behaviour is not the only prospect which may persuade a teacher that a particular pupil is unacceptable.

Q. In making arrangements for a school residential visit, we have sent the usual letter to parents, requiring a signed consent for any emergency medical treatment which might be necessary. One family has endorsed the returned form with a statement that they do not authorize the use of blood transfusion on their child. What is our position?

A. I presume that the family you are dealing with belongs to the Jehovah's Witnesses, or to a similar sect, and have a religious objection to blood transfusion.

The important point here is that you have no obligation to take pupils on a residential visit, if you are not willing to do so. It would be perfectly reasonable, for instance, to refuse to take a pupil whose disciplinary record was such that the staff in charge were unwilling to accept responsibility for him or her away from the school environment. Similarly, you have the right to lay down the conditions for the visit and to inform the parents of them. If, say, you intend to operate a curfew to ensure all pupils are in their rooms by 8.30 p.m., the parents can then decide if they want their child to go on a visit for which that is the rule.

The same applies to the Jehovah's Witnesses. Suppose there were to be a serious accident and their child were to be taken to hospital for emergency surgery, requiring blood transfusion. If the parents are not immediately available, is it reasonable for the teacher in charge to deny the blood transfusion and perhaps occasion the pupil's death? No teacher should have to accept such a heavy burden of responsibility and a written disclaimer is not sufficient to protect him or her morally, whatever might be said in law.

The fact is that parents who send a children on a residential visit in the care of teachers do so under the terms which the school lays down in advance and cannot dictate separate conditions of their own, unless the teachers are willing to accept them. Some variations may be acceptable, but I do not believe that this particular one is and I would advise the school to inform the parents concerned that their stipulation is unacceptable. If they insist upon it, then, with regret, their children cannot be included in the party.

Having agreed the number and composition of the party, the next issue is the ratio of teachers to pupils needed to provide adequate supervision.

Q. Our school is sending a group of 30 pupils on a residential visit to France. What is the minimum number of teachers which should accompany this party?

A.   There are no rules governing this situation, unless your school is an LEA-maintained school, where the LEA has itself made rules. That apart, the professional judgement of the Head is the determining factor, because he or she has the ultimate responsibility.

A number of factors must be taken into account, including the age of the pupils, whether the party is mixed or single-sex, what the hazards of the journey and activities are likely to be and what the arrangements are at the destination. If it is an exchange party, for instance, where the pupils will disperse to individual homes, the requirement may be different from what it would be for a group staying in a hostel or hotel.

It is a little misleading to talk only of teachers in this context. While it would be expected that the leader would be a teacher, under the direct authority of the Head, others could be responsible adults, including parents, and not teachers. Whoever they are, the Head must be satisfied that the arrangements are such as to provide reasonable control and supervision to ensure the safety and welfare of the pupils. For any party, this must include a fall-back arrangement to cover the illness or injury of the leader.

For a party such as you describe, I should recommend a minimum of two, male and female if the party is mixed and, depending on the itinerary and activities, I would prefer to send at least one more. Taking responsibility for 30 youngsters for 24 hours a day over a number of days is a tiring and demanding business and it is wise planning to allow some free time for the adults on a rota basis.

Most parties are likely to include both girls and boys and proper supervision is required for both.

Q. Is it essential that a mixed party of pupils on a visit should be accompanied by teachers of both sexes?

A. Much depends on the circumstances. There are no laws governing the subject, although some LEAs issue directions or guidelines. Where these exist, they should be followed. It is the Head's responsibility to ensure that all parties taking part in out-of-school activities are properly supervised and the number, qualifications and sex of the supervisors are matters of professional judgement.

In general terms, a supervisor of each sex would be required on a residential visit, although such a provision might not be absolutely necessary in every circumstance with sixth-form students. On a long day-trip, supervisors of both sexes are desirable but, for an outing of short duration, this might not be necessary.

I have deliberately used the term supervisor because it is possible to take responsible adults who are not teachers – parents, for example – in order to provide adequate supervision and care.

Q. This school proposes to send a party of sixth-form students on an adventure course. Only one girl has asked to go and there are 12 boys. Must we send a female member of staff?

A. The appropriate level of supervision is a matter for the Head's professional judgement, having taken into account all the circumstances, including the size and composition of the party, the nature of the activities, the arrangements for accommodation, the experience of the group leaders and so on.

Other things being equal, there is nothing inherently wrong in allowing a girl of sixth-form age to take part without there being a female leader, but I should want to be sure that both she and her parents were fully aware of and accepted the proposed arrangements and that the man in charge fully understood the need to be particularly sensitive to her situation as the sole female participant.

From the Head's point of view, the party leader needs to be experienced and capable of fulfilling the demanding responsibilities, which will include dealing with emergencies and, if abroad, with the local population.

Q. Is it absolutely necessary to send a qualified linguist with any school trip abroad?

A. No, not even to the United States! The provision of staff on overseas visits is a matter for the professional judgement of the Head. He or she must be satisfied that the staff accompanying the party are sufficiently numerous, sufficiently qualified and sufficiently experienced to undertake the responsibility, having taken into account the number of the pupils, their age, their sex, the activities in which they are going to engage, any known hazards, the place where they are going to stay and the duration of the visit.

Obviously, when the visit is to a country where English is not the first language, the Head will need to be satisfied that there is provision for communication in emergency. Having someone in the party who speaks the local language is a great advantage, but it is not essential, provided that there are reasonable alternatives.

There are some activities which will require specialist and qualified supervision and this applies particularly to outdoor activities and sports. In these cases, the specialist qualification may be more important than being a teacher.

Q. We have a problem with supervision of groups at the swimming pool, because we can only spare one teacher to go at a time. Is it permissible to send a sixth-form student who holds a life-saving certificate?

A. As with all matters relating to the supervision of pupils, this is a matter for the professional judgement of the Head. If the Head, and the teacher in charge of the group, are satisfied that the arrangements for supervision are adequate in all the circumstances of the case, then what you propose is perfectly acceptable.

The best test is to apply the 'worst-case scenario': if there were to be a tragic accident, would the Head be able to defend the arrangements as reasonable and satisfactory? For the supervision of swimming, the important qualification for a person of any age is in life-saving and a responsible sixth-form student may be as competent in that respect as anyone else, particularly as the teacher is also present.

In some cases, there may be no direct supervision:

Q. Is it permissible for a sixth-form group to go on a school trip without supervision?

A. The level of supervision for a school party is determined by the professional judgement of the Head, which may have to be defended, in the event of something going seriously wrong.

In most circumstances, one would expect there to be some supervision, even at sixth-form level, although there may well be local activities where students of that age may be trusted to take care of themselves. There are also particular events, such as expeditions under the Duke of Edinburgh's Award Scheme, where close supervision would entirely frustrate the nature of the exercise.

The important point is that everyone concerned, including parents, should be fully aware of the arrangements and of the provision made to deal with emergencies.

The importance of parents being fully informed about the arrangements and giving their consent to their son or daughter taking part is already clear and it would be foolish indeed to disregard their wishes. It would be equally foolish to take their consent for granted.

Q. I have always understood that it was necessary to have parental permission to take children on a trip out of school, especially when this involved public transport, an unusual place and a late return to school. My Head recently insisted that I took a pupil on such a trip, although the parent had failed to return the slip and had not provided the bus fare or the packed lunch. The Head said that she would accept responsibility but did not put this in writing. Who would have been responsible if anything had happened to the pupil? Did the Head have the right to direct me to take the pupil?

A. The Head was taking a considerable risk in allowing this child to take part in the trip. The failure to return the slip may well have been deliberate and an indication that the parent did not give consent. Had anything untoward occurred, the parent might well have had grounds for action against the school.

Your Head is, however, right on another point. The fact that a parent has given permission for a child to take part does not absolve the Head and whoever is in charge of the party from their responsibility to provide proper supervision and attention to the safety and welfare of pupils at a standard which might be expected of a reasonable parent. You, as party leader, accepted your part of that responsibility for the conduct of the trip, while your Head accepted responsibility for the overall arrangements and for ensuring that the rules and regulations covering such matters were properly observed.

On your third point, I am on your side. When a teacher takes responsibility for a school trip, he or she is taking on extra responsibilities beyond the norm. While the Head has the power to direct a teacher to carry out duties off school premises as well as on, a teacher may contend that such a direction is unreasonable, if he or she is unhappy with either the arrangements for the trip or the inclusion on it of a particular pupil. The teacher in charge cannot be absolved from responsibility for what happens during the trip by any declaration to that effect from the Head.

That response introduced another important issue: the standards of behaviour which it is reasonable to expect from pupils in unfamiliar surroundings. This can be a particular problem with parties abroad, where the local customs may be rather different.

Q. What should a leader of a school party travelling abroad do about controlling smoking and drinking by pupils, where the laws of the land are more liberal than those back home?

A. A school party anywhere is under the authority of the school and the control of the party leader. The rules which govern the conduct of pupils on that party are those which the school and the leader lay down. Both pupils and parents need to know what those are and to accept that infringement may lead to disciplinary action.

This does not make it any easier for party leaders, particularly with older pupils, in circumstances which you describe. If it is intended to allow a more relaxed regime, for example by allowing older pupils to take a glass of wine with meals, then the nature of that regime should be explained in advance to parents, so that there is no ambiguity or misunderstanding. Their consent to their offspring's participation in the trip should include an acknowledgement that the rules have been seen and understood.

Even in the best-run parties, there is always the possibility that a pupil will behave so badly that he or she can no longer be tolerated as a member of the group.

Q. During a recent school residential visit to France, the teacher in charge sent one pupil home early, following serious misconduct.

Although the parents were given notice of his return and care was taken to ensure that he was escorted during the journey home, the parents are now threatening legal action against the school. Do they have any grounds for doing so?

A. Probably not. When teachers volunteer to take parties of children on visits, they undertake the responsibilities of the parents for the duration of the trip and they are entitled to expect good standards of conduct from those in their charge. As acting parents, they have the right to impose reasonable sanctions when pupils misbehave.

If the misconduct of any pupil is so serious that those in charge no longer wish to accept responsibility for him or her, they have every right to return that pupil to the care of the parents, provided that this is practicable and can be managed with the kind of precautions which were obviously taken in this case. If the parents wish to complain about it, the sensible response would probably be to let the matter be heard by the Disciplinary Committee of the governing body. Although it is not strictly a case for them, the process would at least give the parents the satisfaction that someone had considered their side of the story, although the governors are in no position to insist that teachers must take responsibility for pupils when they are volunteering to run activities in their own time.

No doubt the question of cost will come up too. The parents are not in a position to reclaim as of right any of the money which was paid for the journey, because the contract was broken by the pupil, through bad behaviour, and not by the school. The school might wish, however, to refund *ex gratia* any actual saving which accrued as a result of the pupil being sent home, having made a reasonable deduction for administrative costs.

Misbehaviour can affect the innocent bystander as well as the pupil and this, too, can cause complications.

Q. During a field trip in the countryside, one of our pupils, disobeying the party leader, went onto private land and damaged the property of the landowner. The school has received a claim for £300 in damages. Who is responsible, the pupil, his father, the teacher in charge, the school or the local authority?

A. Although the pupil must be held responsible for both the disobedience and the damage and be suitably punished on both counts, this will be of minor interest to the person whose property has been damaged. He will want his bill paid.

The teacher in charge is responsible for exercising reasonable supervision, having regard to the age of the pupils and the circumstances in which they were working. The Head will wish to be satisfied that nothing was lacking in this respect. If it was, it may be necessary to consider some disciplinary action against the teacher.

The school, and in practical terms, the Head is responsible for ensuring that all school trips are properly arranged and run in accordance with clearly stated and understood school policies. This includes making sure that adequate insurance is taken out to cover risks of personal accident and injury to pupils and staff and third-party liability.

The local authority is responsible for advising schools on their policies in these matters and also for any collective liability which they have for all their employees, whether covered by insurance or not. They also provide legal services to which claims of this nature should be referred as a matter of course.

The most likely outcome of this case is that, unless the landowner had been negligent in caring for his property, the LEA will accept that there is a legitimate claim, which should be met by passing it to the insurance company which issued the policy covering the trip in question. If there was no such policy, the Head should expect a rocket and the LEA will probably settle *ex gratia* or advise the school to do so.

The responsibility of party leadership extends to the arrangements which are made for the transportation and accommodation of the pupils. Careful advance planning and checking are essential.

Q. The recent tragic case raises the question of whether school party leaders ought to visit centres abroad in advance of the party going there. This would be expensive, but is it necessary?

A. In an ideal world, this might be desirable, but it is unlikely to be practicable in many cases. One has to accept the terms and conditions set out by the travel company or by the management of the accommodation as the basis for deciding to go there. There is nothing to stop the party leaders asking all relevant questions until they are satisfied and obtaining the answers in writing.

The key duty of the party leader, however, is to check out all the important details on site as soon as the party arrives and to insist that any point of concern is promptly dealt with.

Q. On a school ski trip, we found that the main entrances to the pension where we were lodged were kept locked, with the only access and exit being provided by way of steep stairs and the cellars. I was subsequently told that, had there been an accident, I could, as party leader, have been prosecuted by the Health and Safety Executive. What should I have done?

A. This is an astonishing situation and demonstrates, I am afraid, that there are still some very dubious operators in the field of school travel. It is vital to ensure that you deal with an operator with a proven record of quality, with experience of school parties, and in membership of ABTA.

The ultimate responsibility, however, was undoubtedly yours. First of all, you should have required details of the nature of the accommodation in advance and satisfied yourself, as far as you reasonably could, that it was appropriate for your party. If, having done that, you had discovered on arrival that the conditions were other than promised, you should have presented the tour operator with an immediate ultimatum: either to provide what had been contracted for or to take the party home at once.

If the problem was essentially with the proprietor of the *pension*, such a threat might well have been effective and, if not, a visit to the local authority in the area might well have done the trick. Your absolute refusal to allow your party to stay in a potentially dangerous situation should have been a powerful bargaining card.

The warning you were given after the event was a proper reminder that you, as party leader, are responsible for the safety and welfare of the pupils placed in your charge and, if you see a situation where your ability to fulfil that responsibility is threatened, it is your duty to act.

Q. On a recent school trip to France, the teacher in charge became concerned about the standard of driving of the coach, due, she

thought, to the fact that the driver was overtired. She took no action.
Do you think she was right?

A. Without more detailed information, it is impossible to say. I can only offer some general observations. The first duty of a teacher is the care and safety of the pupils and, if this teacher had decided that the driver's performance was such as to place the pupils at risk, she should have ordered him to stop and to rest until she felt it was safe to continue. If he had refused to accept that order, she should have contacted the owners of the coach at the first available opportunity thereafter.

Drivers of coaches are subject to strict regulations covering the length of time they are allowed to drive without rest and, if there was reason to believe that these regulations were being broken, the teacher should have reported her suspicions to the police, either at the time or on their return home. All coaches are obliged to carry tachographs, which enable a check to be made.

In any event, the fact that the teacher was unhappy with the standard of driving should have been reported to the coach company. One can well understand that the teacher did not wish to appear foolish by making an unnecessary fuss, but it is far better to do that than to have to live with the knowledge that one failed to act to avert a potentially serious accident.

In spite of every regulation and precaution, dreadful accidents do happen and they always receive publicity. Sometimes, those in charge have been at fault and sometimes they are entirely blameless. Whatever the case, they will feel a sense of failure and guilt for what has happened. They do not always receive the sympathy and support they deserve.

Q. I was disturbed to read in the local press that a coroner had criticized a school following an unfortunate incident involving the death of a pupil off the school premises. From my personal knowledge, I believe that these comments were entirely unwarranted. Does the school have any redress?

A. It is one of the features of the English legal system that judges and coroners enjoy the privilege of making observations in relation to cases before them to which those who feel injured or offended thereby have no right of reply. Such judicial utterances often attract the interest of the press, as they did in this case.

Most judges and coroners are well aware of their responsibilities in such matters and are very careful about what they say, and there are many instances when such pronouncements are welcome because they draw attention to important issues such as safety procedures. Where such pronouncements do cause annoyance or embarrassment, it is not only the judge or, as in this case, the coroner who is at fault. The press, in reporting what has been said, should also have regard to fairness by inviting the aggrieved party to comment on it and so offer an alternative version. If this was not done, the Head or the Chairman of Governors of the school concerned should have offered the press a statement giving their side of the case. Beyond that, I am afraid that there is very little else that can be done. The only consolation is to say that most schools suffer experiences of this sort at one time or another and that, in the great majority of cases, today's story is tomorrow's fish and chip wrapping.

Finally, Heads in particular should remember that, in arranging school journeys, a great deal of money may change hands and every school should have well-understood procedures to ensure that all funds are properly and securely handled and that all accounts are produced and audited. It is also worth noting that not every teacher does it just for the love of it:

Q. At my school, all school trips are run by the same teacher, who is also the travel agent, making a profit from the service he provides. Is this practice acceptable?

A. Were I the Head, or a governor, of your school, I should want to look into this situation very carefully indeed.

I should wish to know, first of all, whether the pupils who were taking part in trips were getting as good a value for their parents' money as could be obtained anywhere else. Secondly, I should wish to know whether this agency was a member of ABTA, with the protection and cover that membership of that association provides.

Next, I should wish to be sure that the activities of this teacher, as travel agent, were entirely divorced from his work as a teacher, in no way impinging on the time for which he is paid a salary by his employer. I should not wish him to transact any business in school nor use the school's facilities in the furtherance of his agency work. I should not wish him to accompany, as a teacher, any school party which he had organized and I should, in any case, be concerned about a possible conflict of interest were anything to go badly wrong on one of these trips.

If I were satisfied on all counts, I should have to concede, in the end, that there was nothing illegal about the operation, although I confess that I should still feel uncomfortable about it. It has to be said, however, that many of the organizations specializing in school travel started out in a similar way to the enterprise which you describe. Some of them have become very successful and enabled their founders to leave teaching for a more lucrative career.

16

Managing with the parents

The relationship between teachers and parents has always generated tension. Neither can do without the other, but neither entirely trusts the other to do the right thing. The ideal is partnership and cooperation, and this is achieved far more often than many people would believe, but for some the situation is one of armed neutrality at best and trench warfare at worst.

Historically, the relationship was always seen as contractual, as indeed it still is for those who choose to educate their children privately. The parents, desiring to have their children educated, hire a tutor, or more commonly a school, to do the job for them. They surrender their offspring voluntarily into the care of the teachers they have chosen, signing over the right to impose discipline as well as learning, and continue the arrangement for as long as they are satisfied that they are getting what they are paying for or, in a few cases, for as long as the school is prepared to accept custody of the children.

In the state sector, the situation is rather different, not least because the state does not give the parents the right not to educate their children. With the exception of the few who can satisfy the state that their own domestic provision is acceptable, the children must be sent to school. The relationship with the school is not contractual and it has increasingly become the subject of legislation imposing rights and duties, the rights mostly going to the parents and the duties to the teachers.

Rights and duties come together in the fundamental question of what is to be taught and, one hopes, learnt. The Education

Reform Act of 1988 introduced the concept of the National Curriculum in England and Wales, giving pupils, and their parents, an entitlement to a curriculum, specified by the state. Until that date, only Religious Education, required by the 1944 Education Act, was a prescribed feature in every school.

Religious Education, however, was the one thing parents could always opt out of and, to this, sex education was added in 1988. This can cause problems.

Q. A parent has sent a written request to the school that her daughter should be withdrawn from Religious Education, but only when the class is learning about religions other than Christianity. Do we have to accede to this?

A. I fear so. Section 9 of the Education Reform Act 1988 says:

> *'If the parent of any pupil in attendance at any maintained school requests that he may be wholly or partly excused ... from receiving religious education given in the school in accordance with the school's basic curriculum ... the pupil shall be so excused accordingly until the request is withdrawn.'*

This seems to be your case exactly, although I can imagine that it will be far from easy for the teacher concerned, who may well, in the course of lessons dealing primarily with Christianity, wish to introduce comparisons with other faiths. We could hardly have the poor pupil popping in and out of the room every five minutes. I suspect that you will have to discuss these practical issues with the parents in order to reach an understanding of how their legitimate request can be sensibly dealt with.

So what happens to the pupil who is withdrawn?

Q. If parents withdraw a pupil from Religious Education, does the school have an obligation to provide an alternative?

A. No. The Education Act 1993 allows parents to withdraw children from RE and they may arrange for them to receive the alternative of their choice elsewhere or, if that is not practicable, at the school. The governing body must provide facilities for this, if requested, provided that they are put to no additional expense in so doing.

If no alternative is provided by the parents, the school has no greater duty than that of normal supervision and care, while the children remain within the school.

In the case of sex education, the right to withdraw pupils does not extend to those aspects of reproduction, human or otherwise, which are included in the National Curriculum in Science.

Q. I have received an instruction from parents that their child must not attend any sex education lessons. Must I comply with this?

A. Up to a point, you must. Parents have the legal right to have their children withdrawn from sex education lessons in the context of what is commonly called 'Personal and Social Education', that is to say those areas of sex education which are concerned with sexual relationships. The right does not extend to the biological aspects of human reproduction, which form part of the National Curriculum in Science.

You would be wise to point out this distinction to the parents in order to avoid misunderstandings.

Religion, like sex, can occur in various parts of the curriculum, but there are limits to what parents can demand:

Q. The governors have received a request from parents that two pupils from the same family should be withdrawn from any lessons where computers are used. We understand that this is related to a particular religious sect. Should we agree?

A. No. Parents have no right to withdraw children from the normal curriculum provided by the school, except from religious education or sex education.

There is at least one minority sect which takes this view about computers and schools would, no doubt, wish to handle the issue in as sympathetic a manner as possible. The law is clear, however, and these parents cannot deny their children access to this important aspect of modern education, except by having them educated privately.

For some parents, it isn't the subject they object to, it is the teacher:

Q. A parent has written to say that he is instructing his son not to attend History lessons, because he does not like the way the teacher has treated the boy. As Head, I have investigated the complaint against the teacher and I have told the parent that there is no substance in his allegation. Must I accept his request?

A. No. If we were to accept that parental choice extended to the right to choose the teachers as well as the school, the result would be chaos. Only in the case of Religious Education does a parent have this right and it relates to the subject and not to the teacher.

You have to inform this parent, if necessary through the mediation of an Education Welfare Officer, that his instruction to his son is invalid: the boy must attend all the lessons to which he is assigned on the timetable. If he fails to do so, he might well have to be excluded from the school. If persuasion fails, the only remedy open to the parent is to ask the governors to investigate his complaint. If that gives him no satisfaction, he may well have to withdraw his son and send him to another school, where the teachers are more to his liking.

What many parents really care about in the end is results and especially results of public examinations. The school is interested, too, but there is plenty of scope for disagreement:

Q. A parent has told the Head that he does not want his son to be entered for the GCSE examination in the subject for which I have prepared him over the past two years. The lad has a good chance of getting a decent grade. Can we disregard the father's opinion?

A. Paragraph (2)(b) of Section 117 of the Education Reform Act 1988 removes the obligation imposed on the governing body to enter a pupil for an examination for which he has been prepared in the school if 'the parent requests in writing that the pupil should not be entered for that examination'.

Your only recourse, I am afraid, is to persuasion.

The odds are not always stacked in the parents' favour:

Q. Can parents insist that their child be entered for an examination at a higher level than the school considers appropriate, given that they are willing to pay for the entry?

A. This is a subject on which the Parents' Charter is positively misleading, in that it claims that parents do have a right to have their children entered for examinations.

The legal position is set out in Section 117 of the Education Reform Act 1988. The governing body is required to enter each pupil for each prescribed examination for which he has been prepared at the school, '*at such time as they consider appropriate*'. They are, however, exempted from that duty if they consider 'that there are educational reasons in the case of that particular pupil for not entering him'.

The parents' case is doubly flawed here, in that Section 106(5) of the same Act makes it illegal for a school to charge for an examination entry for a pupil who has been prepared for the examination at the school. Given Section 117, even a 'voluntary contribution' to the school funds would not buy the parents the right of entry.

Q. This school is trying to recover the examination entry fee from the parents of a boy, whose parents insisted he should be entered, in spite of the fact that he failed to complete the coursework requirement. The parents are refusing to pay. Are they right?

A. No, they are not. This issue is very clearly dealt with in Section 108 of the Education Reform Act 1988:

> '*Where ... the governing body.... have paid any fee in respect of the entry of a registered pupil at the school for a public examination in any syllabus for that examination ... and the pupil fails without good reason to meet any examination requirement for that syllabus requirement ... that body ... may recover the amount of the fee from the pupil's parent.*'

Furthermore, it is for the body which paid the fee to determine whether the pupil had good reason for the failure.

The parents have no case for refusing to pay and, if they persist, a referral to the Small Claims Court is an inexpensive way of enforcing payment.

Normally, however, there can be no question of the parents paying for examination entries:

Q. *I have received a request for payment of my daughter's A level entry fees and the Head of her school (voluntary-aided) says that a charge can be made if the school does not believe she will pass. Her 'mock' predicted grades are CDD. Is this legal?*

A. No. This matter is dealt with in the Education Reform Act 1988. Section 106(5) states quite categorically:

> 'No charge shall be made in respect of the entry of a regis-
> tered pupil at any maintained school for any prescribed
> public examination in any syllabus for that examination for
> which the pupil has been prepared at the school.'

Section 117 of the Act obliges the governing body to enter pupils for the examinations 'at such time as they consider appropriate', but exempts them from that obligation if they 'consider that there are educational reasons ... for not entering him'.

You have every right, therefore, to challenge the Head in this matter. If he or she does not believe a pupil stands any chance of passing, he or she may decide, if empowered to do so by the governing body, not to enter that pupil for the examination. If, because of parental pressure, that decision is reversed, the school must still pay the fees, as Section 106(5) makes clear.

The only possible escape might be that the Head agrees to make the entry because the parent agrees to make a voluntary contribution to the school funds equal to the cost of the entry. I doubt very much that such a practice would stand up under challenge in circumstances such as yours.

Getting entries out of the way is not the end of the matter:

Q. A parent has complained that a member of my staff allowed an A level examination paper to start early, to the disadvantage of his son. What should I do about this?

A. Assuming the facts to be correct, you have two things to do.

If you have good reason to suppose that the student's result could have been affected by this mistake, you should report the facts to the examination board and ask whether special consideration might be given to him.

The teacher concerned has committed a breach of the examination board's regulations and, unless there are extenuating circumstances which excuse the error, disciplinary action in the form of an oral warning may well be appropriate. It is important to remember that, in these circumstances, the school is acting as the agent of the examination board, which is entitled to expect that its regulations should be strictly enforced. If the breach was serious, the board may well seek an assurance that appropriate action has been taken.

Then there are the results and it is probably fortunate that the examination boards allow appeals only from schools and not from parents, although some schools will appeal on behalf of a parent, if the latter is ready to pay the appropriate fee. Information from the boards, however, is supplied to the school, not to the parents:

Q. Our school has obtained a report from the examination board on the performance of our candidates in a particular subject last summer. One parent is demanding to see it. Has she the right?

A. Schools not infrequently seek reports from the board when a particular set of results seems to be seriously out of line with what teachers had been expecting, or with results in other subjects. The information so gained can be helpful to a Head, who needs to know that the teachers are doing their job properly, and to teachers, who need to know whether they have fallen short in their preparation or have simply been let down by their students.

The information provided by the board is for those professional purposes and it is not a report on the performance of individual students. There is a separate process for reviewing the marking of an individual.

Parents do not have a right to see professional reports of this kind, which are general in their nature and do not identify individual performances. How the Head deals with the parental complaint is, therefore, a matter of professional judgement. If the report reveals serious weaknesses, the Head may wish to share it with the governing body, in order to seek support for remedial action.

Schools are also interested in publishing their results, especially if they are good:

Q. The parents of one of our pupils have refused to allow the school to publish their son's GCSE results in the local paper. We have been publishing lists of individual results for years: can they insist on this?

A. Yes. The school has every right to publish the general summary of its results, but the results of the individual candidate are their own.

Most people would not think to question this and local papers are very keen to publish all the names, presumably because it sells more copies. Nevertheless, the wishes of this family should be respected.

Parents who are dissatisfied with the school, for whatever reason, fall into two categories, the litigious and the explosive. The former know their rights and will use all possible channels to pursue their complaint. Apart from specific complaints about the delivery of the National Curriculum, or about the provision for Special Educational Needs, for which there are procedures laid down, parents may complain to the governors, to the local education authority or to the Department for Education and Employment.

Special Needs can be a particularly difficult area:

Q. We have a son who is bright and well behaved, but suffers from school phobia. The LEA has only offered home tuition or a special unit for children with learning or behavioural problems. Neither is appropriate. What can we do?

A. Although this column deals mainly with issues of school management, your question does raise issues of interest.

The resources which local authorities have to deal with pupils who, for whatever reason, cannot be accommodated in mainstream schools are very limited and I am not surprised by the poor response to your son's needs.

I assume that, through your own doctor or the LEA, you have already explored the possibly of specialist psychological advice to help your son overcome his phobia, which is clearly the best approach.

It may be that the LEA could be prompted to give further consideration to finding appropriate help for him and, to help you identify possible options, you might care to contact the Advisory Centre for Education (Tel. 0171 354 8321).

Q. A parent who did not believe her child was making sufficient progress at school decided to buy specialist private tuition which took place during school hours. Because of the child's special needs, the school initially cooperated with this scheme. Latterly, however, that support has been withdrawn and the school, supported by the LEA, has insisted that the child should attend school at all times. Does the parent have the right to insist on her choice in this matter?

A. This is a sad case, but I am afraid that the law is on the side of the school and the LEA. It is not possible, unless by agreement, for pupils to enjoy a mix of public and private education in whatever way a parent chooses. It would clearly lead to chaos if parents were allowed to withdraw their children from school whenever they wished to provide their own alternative.

You do not mention whether this child has been made the subject of a Statement of Special Educational Needs. It sounds as if that might be appropriate in this case and, if it were, the child's special needs would be spelt out in the statement. The LEA would then be responsible for ensuring that provision was made, either within the school or elsewhere, for those needs to be met. In that context, it might be possible to arrange something along the lines of the scheme which the parent wants. The LEA, however, has the right to decide what the provision should be and is open to legal challenge only if it can be demonstrated that the provision is inappropriate or inadequate to meet the stated needs.

Q. A parent has asked the school to agree to her daughter, an ME sufferer, attending school on a part-time basis for specific subjects only. We are resisting this, because we do not believe that it is in the pupil's interests and because we are concerned that she will not be following the full National Curriculum. What would you advise?

A. You are quite right in insisting on the priority of the pupil's interests. The difficulty lies in establishing what they are.

The first thing you need is a clear medical statement about this girl. If need be, you can ask for her to be examined by the LEA Medical Officer. Her fitness to attend school is something for her doctor to determine, not her mother, and, if the doctor advises that a partial return to school would be an aid to recovery, then you should give that serious consideration. You might well discuss it in terms of a planned programme leading towards a full timetable.

Although you are right to be concerned about the National Curriculum, the cumbersome process of disapplication needs only to be considered if the condition looks likely to persist for an extended period.

Handling parental complaints is always a tricky matter for both Heads and governing bodies:

Q. Does a parent who has a complaint against a school, or against an individual teacher, have the right to be heard by the governing body?

A. No. Obviously, any person has the right to lodge a complaint and ought to receive a response from any responsible public body. It is, however, for the governing body itself to determine what that response should be and whether or not the complainant should be heard in person by all, or any, of the governors.

Many governing bodies would make it possible for a complainant to meet a parent-governor, or perhaps the Chairman or Vice-Chairman, but it would be unusual to agree to a meeting with the full governing body. Most governing bodies are rightly careful not to be seen as an alternative channel for petty griev- ances, which ought properly to be directed to the Head, but willing, nevertheless, to consider representations from those who remain dissatisfied after taking the complaint through the appropriate channels first.

Any complainant who believes that a school, or its governing body, has acted unlawfully, does, of course, have the right to challenge the action in court.

The litigious cause many problems, but the explosive can be more dramatic:

Q. When we excluded a badly behaved boy, his father went to the local newspaper, alleging that his son had been seriously bullied, that the teachers had ignored it and had mistreated his son. The paper carried the story on its front page. What should we do?

A. Keep your nerve. This kind of retaliation may well be a way of avoiding facing the reality of the bad behaviour of the son. If the exclusion was justified, the parent's response does not make it any less so and the normal procedures should take their course.

It is disappointing that the paper should publish the story, without seeking your version of it. You will need to conduct an investigation to ensure that there is nothing in the parent's allegations which would stand up to scrutiny and then to issue a statement to the press, denying the fact of bullying in this instance and outlining the school's policy on bullying generally.

You will not wish to refer to the pupil by name, but you may wish to include something in your statement to the effect that the parent who made the allegation is due to have a meeting with the school to discuss incidents relating to his son. As always in such cases, it is necessary, as far as possible, to avoid allowing the actions of the parents influence what needs to be done for the pupil.

When meeting the parent, the two issues should be kept entirely separate. Give a calm and reasoned response to the allegation of bullying and then discuss what is to be done about the exclusion. It would probably be as well to have a reliable witness present at this interview.

Q. I asked the parents of a seriously disruptive eight-year-old to meet me to discuss the situation. When I described the problem, the father lost his temper, rather like his son, and stomped out. What should I do?

A. It rather looks as if this little boy is using his father as a role-model and this is precisely the message which the latter has to receive. This case is clearly going to call for a good deal of patient hard work, perhaps beginning with the Educational Welfare Officer, who should be given the task of persuading the father to return, as they say, to the negotiating table.

He has to be convinced that you are interested in the education of his son and that progress can only be achieved if you both work together on an agreed plan. Maybe a meeting with the father on his own or neutral territory would be easier for him than a confrontation at school. You do not mention the boy's mother: is there a way in which she might help to calm down the situation?

There are times when war breaks out on both sides:

Q. At a recent parents' evening, a parent caused a major scene by shouting, knocking over furniture and criticizing the school in very intemperate language before storming out. It transpired that the teacher with whom he had been speaking had suggested that the son's poor behaviour was a consequence of a lack of home control. Both the parent and the teacher are demanding apologies: neither will give one. What can I do?

A. This looks like a case for the UN, or perhaps ACAS! Certainly, the way ahead is likely to be through mediation rather than further confrontation and you do hold some cards in your hand to help you to bring this about.

The teacher is, in some respects, the easier to deal with. However well-based his or her comments may have been, it was not his or her place to make them and to have done so betrays a lack of professional judgement which might warrant an oral warning to be administered. Naturally, you have no wish to take such a measure in this case, but it may well be helpful if a member of your senior management team takes the teacher on one side to point out that continued intransigence might leave you with no alternative but to require an apology to be given and to take disciplinary action if it is refused.

At the same time – and delivering the other side of the bargain – you might wish the Education Welfare Officer to call on the parent at home to discuss the issue, pointing out that the level of the undoubted provocation was not such as to justify such a public and disruptive outburst. He should be told that you would be well within your rights to debar him from entering the school premises, without prior appointment, a step you would be reluctant to take for the sake of the pupil, whose well-being is the concern of both parties.

You will note particularly that I have suggested the use of 'go-betweens' to do the negotiation. Your own position is such that, if you tried to do it yourself, however gently, it would be seen as threatening. In any case, you have to keep clear of the talking, in case you are obliged to take the very actions you are hoping to avoid.

Whether these strategies will work depends, of course, on the temperaments of the contending parties and the diplomatic skills of well-chosen mediators, but that is what the UN and ACAS are all about.

There are times when it might seem more appropriate to punish the parents, if only one could:

Q. What can I do about parents who telephone, write or come into school and use foul and abusive language to teachers, whenever their child is disciplined? Can I exclude a child on the basis of parents' misconduct?

A. Virtually every school has an experience of this sort at some time, usually brought about by the incapability of inadequate parents to cope with the demands of relating with teachers. Their defensiveness about their child's misbehaviour and their own inability to deal with it are covered by aggressive behaviour.

The explanation does not make it in any way acceptable, but it may help in devising strategies to deal with it. Very often, the most likely way forward is to enlist the help of an Education Welfare Officer, or other outside party, who can meet the parents on their own ground or at a neutral venue and patiently bring them to reason. It sometimes works, at least until the next time.

Where remedial action fails, the school may be obliged to tell the parents that they are not to enter school premises, other than to see the Head and by prior appointment. If they fail to comply, they may be treated as trespassers and, if need be, removed by the police. Letters should be answered with patience and restraint and telephone calls intercepted by a responsible person.

The Head may find it helpful, in some instances, to arrange for a meeting with the Chairman, or a small committee of governors, who can explain to the parents what their responsibilities are and how their particular behaviour cannot be tolerated. It can be explained to them that they have chosen to send their child to this school and, by so doing, have accepted the conditions set out in the school prospectus. If these are not acceptable to them, they have the undoubted right to seek a school which is more congenial to them.

It would be quite wrong, in my view, to exclude the pupil for the misdemeanours of the parents. The child is probably acutely embarrassed by their behaviour and hopelessly confused between affection for them and respect for the school. His or her welfare must be the central concern in all the efforts made to resolve the problem.

Q. Once a pupil has been permanently excluded, can the parents insist that the school provides work for him or her to do at home?

A. It is common practice for schools to provide work for pupils who have been temporarily excluded, if only to make the point that they should not be sitting around in idleness.

A permanent exclusion is only finally so when the procedures of hearings and appeal have been exhausted. It could be argued, therefore, that the provision of some work in the interim period was not inherently unreasonable. It might also be a good indication of the parents' willingness to cooperate with the school, should reinstatement be agreed. It is up to the school to decide what is reasonable in the circumstances.

Punishment, as in this last case, is central to most disputes between schools and parents, some of whom would like to question the school's right to punish at all:

Q. I am a primary school teacher who is being challenged by a parent because I have punished her child for misbehaviour in school. This parent says that I should discuss the matter with her before I punish the child. Can she insist on this?

A. No. It has long been established that, when a pupil is in school, the teacher is *in loco parentis*, that is, taking over the role of the parent in caring for the child. This caring includes taking steps to control his or her behaviour in a manner which might be expected of a reasonable parent and this, when exhortation and admonition have failed, means the imposition of moderate and reasonable punishment, appropriate to the nature of the misconduct.

The concept of 'a reasonable parent' is not specific: it is not the parent, whether reasonable or not, of any one child, but rather the broad view which society at large takes of what might be expected of parents. Thus, your aggrieved parent cannot argue that the treatment accorded to her child should differ from the normal practice, simply because she happens to disagree with either the school's policy or with the measures which you have taken in dealing with a particular instance of misconduct.

So, this parent cannot insist that you discuss punishing her child before the event, although she is, of course, entitled to an explanation of what you have done and why, if she wishes to raise the matter afterwards. If she is dissatisfied by your explanation, she has the right to complain to your Head or to the governing body, but her complaint must be not that you have no right to punish the child, but that you have done so unreasonably.

In recent times, the debate has, on occasions, moved away from the rights of parents and moved on to the rights of the child, or young person. Not every parent is happy about this:

Q. During the programme of vaccination against measles, a thirteen-year-old pupil accepted the vaccination, in spite of the fact that his mother had returned the form, indicating that she did not wish him to do so. She is now complaining to the school for allowing it. What is the legal position?

A. This has nothing to do with the school. The school carried out its legal responsibility to provide a room where the health authority could carry out its function and facilitated their work by arranging for the distribution and collection of the relevant information and forms. The treatment itself and all decisions related to it are exclusively the responsibility of the health authority.

While the mother's complaint should be referred to the health authority, I fear that she will not receive much comfort there either. The Children Act created the concept of the 'mature minor', that is, a young person who is deemed capable of taking decisions about personal medical treatment on his or her own account, regardless of parental wishes. In practice, this status is attained from about 12 years old.

This concept is most commonly applied in cases of teenage pregnancies, but, as was upheld by the then Secretary of State for Health herself, it also applies to vaccinations and other medical procedures.

I do have a residual concern in this matter that nurses and doctors should not apply undue pressure to young people in these situations. One would like to think that they were given the opportunity to reflect on their position and, where possible, to resolve their differences with their parents.

Q. A girl in Year 10 has recently had an abortion and she has told her form tutor about it. She does not want her parents to know what has happened, but both her tutor and I, as Head, feel we are betraying the trust which parents place in us by not telling them. Equally, we are worried about their reaction, should they discover subsequently that we knowingly concealed the information. What do you advise?

A. It is a tribute to the quality of the relationship which teachers often establish with pupils that it is not uncommon for pupils to confide in teachers their most serious problems. To betray that confidence would destroy the relationship and it is something that any teacher should be most reluctant to do.

In this case, it is certainly not necessary, for two specific reasons:

1   The Children Act confers the right on adolescents to take a measure of responsibility for decisions affecting their own lives and this decision falls within that legislation.
2   The abortion was a personal and professional matter involving the girl and the doctor who carried out the operation. The

question of informing the parents rests with them and the doctor's professional code of ethics does not require such disclosure. It has nothing to do with the school.

Should the parents ever complain, they would have to be told that, although the school had advised the girl to tell them, her right to do as she wished had to be respected.

Q. One of our sixth-form girls has left her home because her parents have said that they will not support her in her aspirations to go to university. She has told us where she is now living but has asked us not to reveal this information to her parents. Should I, as Head, respect her confidence?

A. Yes. The Children Act gives children rights over their own lives and that certainly includes students over 16, who are well able to understand what they are doing and to take responsibility for their actions.

One is bound to have much sympathy with this girl's position and there is no reason for you to act in a way which would both forfeit her trust in you and possibly damage her future educational prospects.

In spite of all the hard cases, it is, fortunately, partnership which wins in the end, although schools must always remember not to push their luck too hard in exploiting the willingness of the majority of parents to do all they can for the school their children attend:

Q. The voluntary-aided school attended by my children has always sought voluntary contributions from parents. The governors have recently adopted the practice of asking for £35 per child per term and the request looks very much like a bill. Is this legal?

A. It is not illegal, because, as I see in the copy you sent me, the small print still makes it clear that what is being sought is a voluntary contribution. It does, none the less, smack of sharp practice.

While one has every sympathy with hard-pressed schools in seeking to top up their depleted coffers, to the undoubted advantage of the pupils, they should take care not to put undue pressure upon parents to meet what are, in your case, quite substantial contributions.

The proper place to raise this matter is through the PTA, if the school has one, or through elected parent-governors, if it does not. If your reservations about the style of fund-raising are shared by others, the governors may well be persuaded to adopt a less pressurizing approach.

Even in the best of partnerships, one must take care to ensure that things do not go terribly wrong. Enthusiasm can bring its own problems to the unwary:

Q. Parents have offered to repaint some classrooms and to provide additional power points. What are the legal or insurance implications of using such voluntary labour?

A. There are two aspects to this question: the protection of those engaged on the work and the health and safety of pupils and other users of the school premises.

As far as the volunteers are concerned, one would not wish to see them as victims of uninsured accidents, nor as defendants in actions for negligence. It would be sensible, therefore, if the work which they undertake is under the umbrella of an organization, such as a PTA or Friends of the School, which can take out appropriate insurance cover against any contingent risks.

One also needs to be satisfied that any work which they undertake satisfies appropriate safety standards. With routine painting, this may not be a serious problem, although there might be issues relating to lead-free paint in an area used by very young infants or nursery classes. With electrical work, the need to observe standards is obvious. In every case, it would be wise to seek the advice of the Local Education Authority and to have both plans and completed work inspected by a qualified person.

17

Records, reports and files

It is not so very many years ago that schools were left very much to their own devices in almost everything connected with reports and records. Until 1956, there was a duty imposed on the Head to keep a log-book, recording staff absences and significant events in the life of the school. Local Education Authorities required various matters to be attended to in relation to their functions, but, for the rest, including such things as school reports and records, schools were left to do whatever they wished.

The revolution which has changed everything over the past 20 years is not just the technological revolution, which has made all sorts of things possible which could never have been done before, but also the political revolution, which has created a huge central-ized legislative burden, which schools struggle hard to keep up with.

Some changes have been highly desirable and have arisen from the establishment of the right of any individual to know about personal information held on files anywhere. The law has given everyone the right to see files which are held about them and to question the accuracy of the information held. For children, their rights are exercised by their parents.

Q. A parent has asked to see her daughter's school file. Is she entitled to do this? Am I allowed to decide whether to do so or not?

A. Parents have every right to see the files kept on their children and you have no alternative but to comply with her request. It follows from this that care should be taken with the maintenance of all files on pupils so as to exclude from them ephemeral material or unsubstantiated comments. Copies of confidential references may be extracted from the file before allowing access but all other records should be available for inspection.

The question of what can be excluded from the file shown to the parents is also laid down by law:

Q. Now that parents have the right to see the school files on their children, what can I do about a letter from the Social Services Department about a particular pupil, which relates to a suspicion of child abuse within the family?

A. As far as disclosure is concerned, you need do nothing. Reports of this nature are specifically excluded from the obligation under the Education (School Records) Regulations 1989.

All you have to do, if the parents ask to see the file, is to ensure that this letter and any related material is removed before the parents see it. They need not be aware that it exists.

So far so good, but there is also the problem, in this age of collapsing marriages and single-parent families, of defining who is a parent. The general answer has to be that one has to be inclusive of both natural parents and step-parents, regardless of who has actual custody of the child.

Q. The father of one of our pupils has told me that he has separated from his wife and a divorce is pending. He wishes to be kept fully informed about his daughter's progress and, if necessary, to meet her teachers. How should I respond?

A. It should be a cardinal rule for all schools not to become involved in matrimonial or custodial disputes and they need to be on their guard against parents who, regrettably, seek to make use of the school in pursuit of their own ends.

The Children Act 1989 gave separated and divorced parents shared parental responsibility for their children and they are expected to specify the arrangements for the children at the time of the separation or divorce. Parents who were divorced before the Act was passed have parental responsibility, but they must not act in ways which are inconsistent with a previously existing custody order.

Unless there is a court order to the contrary, all those who have parental responsibility must be treated equally by schools. This means that they have the right to vote in the election of parent-governors and for a change of status of the school, to receive school reports and to inspect the pupil's personal file, if they wish to do so. The Act also provides that both parents are entitled to be consulted about important decisions about their children.

If parents are unable to agree on any issue, they must resolve it themselves, if necessary by applying to the court. The school is entitled to ask the parents for clear information on such matters as where the child is normally resident and who will sign absence notes and other routine communications.

Of course, some students are adults well before they leave school:

Q. Must a school pass the 'A' level results of an eighteen-year-old to her parents?

A. Under the Education (Individual Pupils' Achievements) (Information) Regulations, 1993 (SI 3182), the school has a duty to provide parents of a pupil under eighteen information about external examination results. This duty does not extend to students over the age of eighteen, although the results do form a part of the School Leaver's Report, which the school must issue to the student.

In its Circular 16/93, the Department of Education says that the headteacher has discretion to send the report to the parents of those over eighteen. Where there is any doubt about the matter, it might be wise for the Head to consider the wishes of the student.

The question of files and records arises also when pupils move from one educational establishment to another:

Q. A number of pupils leave our local primary school every year to enter various independent schools. Providing reports on these pupils for their new schools requires much staff time and effort. For the children's sake, one would not wish teachers to refuse to provide reports but could the school charge a fee for the service? We have been advised that this is illegal under the 1944 Education Act but is this a fair interpretation?

A. Your advice is out of date but the answer is broadly the same. This matter is dealt with in the Education (School Records) Regulations 1989, (SI 1261) and in DES Circular 17/89. These regulations were made under Section 218 of the Education Reform Act 1988.

Briefly, these regulations lay down that a school considering the admission of a pupil, whether independent or maintained, may apply in writing for the record of that pupil from the previous school. A response must be given within 15 school days and no charge may be made. Additional copies may be charged for, the fee not exceeding the actual cost of supply.

The school record to which this refers is the curriculum record of the pupil, which must be updated at least once a year, together with any other educational records which the school has kept, including a teacher's record, although not material which a teacher may have made solely for that teacher's own use. It does not refer to records held on computer, to which the Data Protection Act 1984 applies.

Excluded from the requirement is:

- information supplied by non-employees of the school or LEA;
- information which would identify the source of information or a person, other than the pupil, to whom it relates;
- information relating to child abuse;
- a reference provided to UCAS for entry to higher education.

Although this is all pretty complex, the legal requirement is simply to hand over the records. The law does not require the compilation of a separate or special report. If teachers decide to do this because they feel it is in the children's interest, that is very praiseworthy but they are not obliged to do so.

Q. As Head of an independent school, I have recently written to a maintained school, seeking a report on a pupil whose parents are seeking to transfer her to us. The Head has replied that the cost of such a report will be £10. Must we pay this?

A. No. The regulations covering access to information in schools (SI 1261 (1989)) make it quite clear that reports on the academic progress of pupils, which are available to parents as of right and free of charge, are equally available to a school which wishes to see them in order to consider admission. The only circumstances where a charge may be levied is where additional copies are required and then the charge may not exceed the actual cost of providing it.

The technological revolution has given added twists to the legal complexities, by setting out a different set of rules with which everyone who stores data on computers must comply.

Q. Is it necessary for the school as well as the LEA to be registered under the Data Protection Act?

A. Yes, I am afraid it is. I believe that efforts were made by interested parties to have the law amended so as to make this multiple registration unnecessary, and so save on the fees, but officialdom has failed to react.

Q. A parent has asked to see the reference which the school has written on his daughter for university entrance. Our records are held on a protected computer file. Am I obliged to allow this, even though it is confidential?

A. The Data Protection Act covers all material held on a computer and therefore cuts across the regulations made under the Education Reform Act. Higher education references are a good example of this. One can have an argument about whether students or their parents should see these anyway, and there are conflicting views, but the law is a muddle.

Under the Education (School Records) Regulations 1989, references of this sort can be withdrawn from the file to which parents have access. However, if they are held on a computer, the Data Protection Act insists that access be given. So, if a school wishes to keep copies of its UCAS references and does not wish parents or students to have access to them, it must print off hard copies and erase the computer files, keeping the record in an old-fashioned file.

Even in the computer age, the paperless office is still not entirely with us and schools have a real problem about retaining archive material:

Q. How long should a school retain records of pupils and staff after they have left?

A. Unless the LEA has made specific rules, there are none and you should have a school policy which serves your own needs.

In the case of pupils, requests for confirmation of external examination results may be received several years later, which suggests that those records need to be kept longer than most. Requests for references do not usually appear after about five years and it is probably safe to dispose of all but the bare bones of records after that time.

For staff, the position is probably similar, although 10 years might be a safer limit in this case. When a change of headship occurs, it is very helpful to a new incumbent not to have to rely entirely on folk memory when answering enquiries and it is useful, therefore, to retain records of names and dates of service over a longer period.

The issue of access to records occurs in a number of contexts, including the divulging of information to outside bodies. The following question has a not very well-hidden agenda about the tensions between schools and FE colleges in some areas:

Q. Are schools obliged to supply FE colleges with lists of pupils' names and addresses so that they can send out their recruitment literature?

A. No. This information is protected by the Data Protection Act and should not be divulged, except with the permission of the individual parents.

On the other hand, schools are obliged by law to distribute the information on behalf of the colleges. The reason for this is that the government was persuaded that some schools were deliberately refusing to do this, thus depriving pupils and parents of information about the full range of educational opportunities available after the end of compulsory education.

Lists of names and addresses are valuable assets in other respects too:

Q. Our school is about to have a ballot for 'opting out'. One of the governors has asked me, as Head, to let him have a copy of the list of parents, so that he can write to them to express his opposition to grant-maintained status. Should I let him have it?

A. Only if he is a parent. The rules governing the conduct of the ballot are very precise and should be followed to the letter.

The governing body has a duty to produce a list of parents of pupils registered at the school and also the electoral roll for the ballot. These two are likely to be exactly the same, except that, in the first case, all parents have to be given the opportunity to have their names removed from the list, if they so wish. They are not, of course, removed from the electoral roll.

The first list, but not the second, must then be made available for inspection by any parent and any parent may also be given a copy of it, although a reasonable fee may be charged for this. The list is not open to inspection by anyone else and no copy may be given to anyone else.

As the governing body has the duty of ensuring that these lists are compiled, presumably by school staff, obviously they may see it – as a body. Individual governors have no more right of access to it than anybody else, unless, of course, they happen also to be parents of registered pupils.

Q. Should the school cooperate with the District Council in supplying the names of students eligible for inclusion on the Electoral Register?

A. It is, of course, the duty of the head of every household to ensure that all those resident in his or her house are registered to vote. It is not the duty of a school to supply names and addresses to the Registration Officer, although it would be helpful to display or circulate any information which he might send out which reminded students of their right to vote and of the need to check that they have been registered.

That question came in while the Community Charge was still being levied and my suspicious mind harboured the thought at the time that this might have been a subtle means of checking the register for the Community Charge, which was no part of the school's business.

Records of quite a different sort were raised by this question:

Q. Must a Head always report to the governors and must the report always be written?

A. Paragraph 30(16) of the *School Teachers' Pay and Conditions of Service Document* imposes on the Head the duty of '... making such reports to (the governing body) in connection with the discharge of his functions as it may properly require either on a regular basis or from time to time'.

The nature, frequency and style of reports is, therefore, a matter to be discussed between the governors and the Head, with a view to establishing a procedure which provides the information and advice to which the former are entitled in a way which best meets their needs. Whatever is agreed, there can be no doubt that the Head must report on matters for which she or he is responsible.

The normal inference of a duty to present a report is that it should be in writing, but this is not an obligation. It certainly saves time, if nothing else, to have extensive reports submitted in writing and in advance, so that governors may have time to study them before they are called upon to take decisions arising from them. At the same time, there will always be issues where the Head judges, and the governors arc happy to accept, that an oral report will be the best method of presentation.

There is one important consideration which should not be overlooked, whichever mode is used, and that is the need to ensure that an accurate record is kept. This can be in the minutes of the meeting or in the form of an adopted written report, which effectively forms part of the minutes.

Minutes and the accuracy thereof are constant sources of bother, especially to those of a legalistic turn of mind. A case could be made for national training courses in writing minutes which are brief, accurate and contain no extraneous matter, but perhaps that would spoil the fun?

Q. Do we have to keep formal minutes of governors' committee meetings? What is their status?

A. When a governing body establishes a committee with a remit to carry out specified functions, and particularly where that remit includes delegated powers of decision making, it is vital that proper minutes are kept, that they are formally approved at a subsequent meeting and that they are laid before the full governing body as a report.

Effectively, these meetings are simply extensions of the full governing body and their records are no less important than the main minutes of which, once reported, they form a part. Key decisions are often taken at committee level and it is essential that they should be accurately recorded.

Q. The record kept of the annual parents' meeting last year was inaccurate in respect of the list of governors who attended. Is there an obligation to keep accurate minutes of these meetings and who is responsible for them?

A. There are no regulations which cover this point and it is therefore up to the governing body to determine what it wishes to do. One would assume that, if they did decide to keep a record, corrections on matters of fact would be accepted, if agreed.

It would, of course, be necessary to keep a record of any resolution which was passed at the meeting, if the meeting was quorate, because the governing body would have the duty to consider it at a subsequent meeting. The rest of the proceedings, which would probably be centred around the governors' report, would not need to be recorded, unless the governors wanted some notes for future reference. The annual meeting is not a business meeting in the usual sense and has no executive function.

Index

R